Beginner

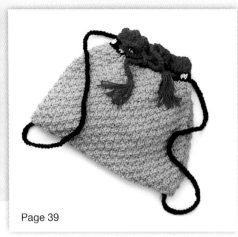

STRIPED BAG
Page 16

LILYPAD BACKPACK
Page 39

Page 39

CONTENTS

MP3 PLAYER AND CELL PHONE CASES
Page 2

MESSENGER BAG
Page 3

T-SHIRT BAG
Page 6

LADY DAY BAG
Page 9

DRAWSTRING BACKPACK
Page 12

BUCKET BAG
Page 13

WASHINGTON SQUARE BAG
Page 15

CARPETBAGGER
Page 17

POLKA DOT FELTED BAG
Page 20

GARTER STRIPE BAG
Page 21

CABLED SHOULDER BAG
Page 37

BAG-ATELLE
Page 40

Easy

CABLED BAG
Page 7

SNOWFLAKE BAG
Page 10

SMALL SHOULDER BAG
Page 14

FELTED SACK
Page 18

SPARKLE CLUTCH
Page 21

DAISY MINI TOTE
Page 22

FELTED WATERMELON TOTE
Page 24

CABLED BACKPACK
Page 25

FELTED COIN PURSE
Page 27

CHAIN LINK BACKPACK
Page 28

PAISLEY CARRY-ALL CARPETBAG
Page 29

PAILETTE BAG
Page 30

MARKET BAG
Page 31

EYE POD PURSE
Page 35

CENTRAL PARK CLUTCH
Page 36

WEEKENDER BAG
Page 38

INDIAN MIRROR BAG
Page 4

BOBBLE BAG
Page 8

FAIR ISLE FELTED TOTE
Page 19

CABLED CARRY-ALL
Page 23

ROSEBUD LACE TRAVEL BAG
Page 26

FELTED DIAMOND BAG
Page 32

EVENING BAG
Page 34

Experienced

Intermediate

MP3 Player & Phone Cases

MEASUREMENTS
MP3 Player Case
• 4" x 4¾"/10cm x 12cm
Cell Phone Case
• 3½" x 5"/9cm x 12.5cm

GAUGE
22 sts and 24 rows to 4"/10cm over St st.
Take time to check gauge.

MP3 PLAYER CASE
BODY
Cast on 18 sts.
Rows 1–6 Work in garter st.
Rows 7–72 Work in St st.
Row 73–78 Work in garter st. Bind off.

I-CORD STRAP
Cast 4 sts onto one dpn. *Knit 1 row.
Without turning the work, slip the sts
back to the beginning of the row. Pull the
yarn tightly from the end of the row. Rep from * until I-cord
measures 40"/100cm. Fasten off.

FINISHING
Fold body in half, wrong sides tog. Sew side seams leaving a
½"/1.5cm space at base on each side. Insert ends of cord into
holes at base. Secure ends and sew cord to sides of piece.

CELL PHONE CASE
Cast on 17 sts.
Rows 1–4 Work in garter st.
Rows 5–68 Work in St st.

Jenny Acheson

Rows 69–78 Sl 1 purlwise wyib, k to end.
Rows 79–92 Sl 1 purlwise wyib, k to last 3 sts, k2tog, k1.
Row 93 Sl 1 purlwise wylb, k2tog, psso.
Change to crochet hook. Ch 8, sl st in base of first ch. Fold piece
wrong sides tog to form a pocket. Work a rnd of sl st around
piece, finish at base of loop. Fasten off and secure ends. Sew
button opposite loop.

MESSENGER Bag

YOU'LL NEED:

YARN ④
14oz/400g, 900yd/850m of any worsted weight wool in purple (MC)
3½oz/100g, 220yd/200m in pink multi (CC)

NEEDLES
Size 10 (6mm) needles *or size to obtain gauge*

ADDITIONAL MATERIALS
Size I-9 (5.5mm) crochet hook
40"/101.5cm of 2"/5cm wide black nylon strapping
Sewing needle and black thread
3½" x 13½"/9cm x 34.5cm piece of ½"/12.5mm thick EVA foam

Jenny Acheson

MEASUREMENTS
• 14" x 11"x 3½"/35.5cm x 28cm x 9cm

GAUGE
15 sts and 19 rows to 4"/10cm in St st.
Take time to check your gauge.

BAG
With MC, cast on 75 sts. Work in St st for 60"/152.5cm. Bind off.

SIDES (make 2)
With MC, cast on 16 sts. Work in St st for 18¼"/46.5cm. Bind off.

FINISHING
Lining up bound-off edges, align one side piece to main bag piece. With CC, crochet tog as foll: 2 sc every 3 rows, 1 sc in each st. Crochet tog down long edge of side, across bottom of side, and back up other long edge of side. Cont working on main piece only, work around flap, join second side to mirror first, work across bound-off edge to beg. Work a rnd of sl st around entire piece.

FELTING
Place bag in washing machine set to hot wash/cold rinse with low water level. Add 1 tablespoon dishwashing detergent and ¼-cup baking soda at beginning of wash cycle. Repeat the cycle, if necessary, until bag is felted to the desired size. Tumble dry on high. Steam block. Fold ends of strap until 2"/5cm and sew to sides of bag. Sew gusset tucks into top edges of sides by bringing corners together. Insert foam base into bag.

INDIAN MIRROR *Bag*

YOU'LL NEED:

YARN ③
1¾oz/50g, 85yd/78m of any DK weight wool in dk grey (A), off white (B), lt green (C), red (D), blue (E), lt purple (F) and mustard yellow (G)

NEEDLES
One pair size 6 (4mm) needles *or size to obtain gauge*
Size 6 (4mm) circular needle, 16"/40cm long

ADDITIONAL MATERIALS
Size F/5 (4mm) crochet hook
Twelve 18mm acrylic "shisha" mirrors
Leather lacing, 34"/86cm for drawstring and 54"/137cm for shoulder strap

each side of next row then every row 9 times more—19 sts. Bind off. Place a yarn marker to mark center bound-off st.

BAG
With circular needle and A, beg and end at center yarn marker, pick up and k 98 sts evenly around outside edge of bottom. Do not join, but turn and work back and forth in rows as foll: k 1 row on WS.

Beg Chart 1
Row 1 (RS) Foll row 1 of chart 1, work first st of chart, work 48 sts of rep twice, work last st of chart. Cont to foll chart in this way through row 37. With B, beg with a p row, work even in St st for 13 rows.
Drawstring eyelet row (RS) K2, *k2tog, yo twice, ssk, k6; rep from *, end last rep k2.
Next row *P to double yo, p into front of first yo, p into back of second yo; rep from *, end p3. Cont with B in St st for 2 rows.

Beg Chart 2
Row 1 (RS) Foll row 1 of chart 2, work first st of chart, work 48 sts of rep twice, work last st of chart. Cont to foll chart in this way through row 20.

MEASUREMENTS
• Approx 11" x 9½"/28cm x 24cm

GAUGE
20 sts and 26 rows to 4"/10cm over St st.
Take time to check gauge.

BAG
BOTTOM
With F, cast on 19 sts. Foll chart for stripes, inc 1 st each side of every row 10 times—39 sts. Work even for 15 rows. Dec 1 st

LINING

Cont in St st, work stripe pat as foll: 3 rows C, 3 rows D, 3 rows E, 3 rows G and 3 rows F. Bind off.

FINISHING

Block to measurements.

EMBROIDERY

Using contrast colors as in photo, embroider small French knots in center of each square around top and lower sections of bag. Using contrast colors, work straight sts around drawstring eyelets (see photo).

CROCHET RINGS

Using contrast colors as in photo, work with crochet hook as foll: Ch 8, join to first ch; to form ring. Ch 1, work 12 sc into ring: Secure, leaving a long end for sewing. Sew ring to center of diamond and slip mirror in place before sewing down completely. Fold over stripe lining at top of bag and sew in place. Sew back seam. Pull shorter leather lacing through drawstring eyelets and knot ends. Pull shoulder strap lacing through center back seam at 2 eyelets. Knot ends.

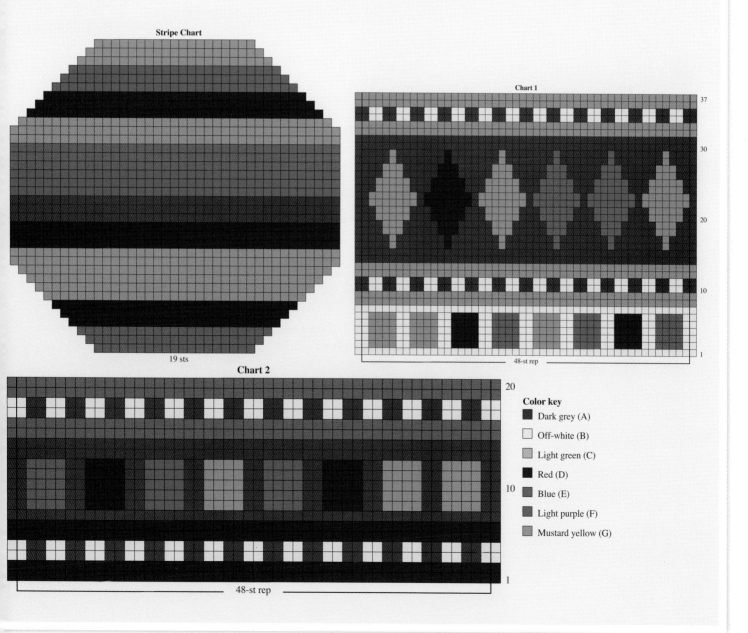

Stripe Chart

19 sts

Chart 1

37
30
20
10
1

48-st rep

Chart 2

20
10
1

48-st rep

Color key

■ Dark grey (A)
□ Off-white (B)
▨ Light green (C)
■ Red (D)
▨ Blue (E)
▨ Light purple (F)
▨ Mustard yellow (G)

T-SHIRT Bag

Paul Amato for LVARepresents.com

YOU'LL NEED:

YARN (6)
240yd/220m, 240yd/220m of any super-bulky weight cotton blend yarn (yarn pictured is t-shirt yarn)

NEEDLES
One size 13 (9mm) circular needle, 24"/60cm long *or size to obtain gauge*
One pair size 11 (8mm) needles

ADDITIONAL MATERIALS
Stitch marker

SLIP STITCH PATTERN (over an even number of sts)
Set-up rnd Purl.
Rnd 1 *Sl 1 wyif, p1; rep from * around.
Rnd 2 *K1, p1; rep from * around.
Rep rnds 1 and 2 for slip stitch pattern.

GARTER RIB (multiple of 5 sts)
Rnd 1 Knit.
Rnd 2 *K3, p2; rep from * around.
Rep rnds 1 and 2 for garter rib.

BAG
With larger needles, cast on 70 sts. Place marker (pm) for beg of rnd and join, being careful not to twist sts. K 1 rnd.

BEG SLIP STITCH PATTERN
Beg with set-up rnd, work in sl stitch pat until rnd 1 has been completed 7 times.
Make one garter ridge as foll: K 1 rnd. P 1 rnd. K 1 rnd.

BEG GARTER RIB
Work in garter rib until piece measures 10½"/26.5cm from beg, end with a rnd 1.

SHAPE BASE OF BAG
Make 2 garter ridges as foll: Purl 1 rnd, knit 1 rnd, purl 1 rnd.
Next (dec) rnd [S2KP, k2, S2KP, k27] twice—62 sts.
Next rnd K to last st, sl st, remove marker, sl st back to LH needle, pm for new beg of rnd.
Next (dec) rnd [S2KP, S2KP, k25] twice—54 sts.
K1, remove marker. Turn bag inside out and with size 11 (8mm) needles, close base of bag with 3-needle bind-off.

HANDLES (make 2)
With size 11 (8mm) needles, cast on 24 sts. Purl 2 rows. Bind off purlwise. Sew to inside of bag using photo as guide.

MEASUREMENTS
• **Circumference** 25"/63.5cm
• **Length** 10½"/26.5cm

GAUGE
12 sts and 16 rows to 4"/10cm over St st using larger needles.
Take time to check gauge.

STITCH GLOSSARY
S2KP Sl 2 sts tog, k1, pass 2 sl sts over the k1.

SPECIAL TECHNIQUE
3-NEEDLE BIND-OFF
1 Hold right sides of pieces together on two needles. Insert third needle knitwise into first st of each needle, and wrap yarn knitwise.
2 Knit these two sts together, and slip them off the needles. *Knit the next two sts together in the same manner.
3 Slip first st on 3rd needle over 2nd st and off needle. Rep from * in step 2 across row until all sts are bound off.

NOTE
Bag is knit in the round from the top down.

CABLED Bag

YOU'LL NEED:

YARN
15¾oz/450g, 330yd/300m of any super-bulky weight wool

NEEDLES
Size 9 (5.5mm) needles *or size to obtain gauge*

ADDITIONAL MATERIALS
Cable needle (cn)
½yd/½m lining fabric (optional)
1 magnetic snap
sewing needle and matching thread

MEASUREMENTS
• 8½" x 10" x 3"/21.5cm x 25.5cm x 7.5cm

GAUGE
12 sts and 24 rows to 4"/10cm over seed st.
Take time to check gauge.

STITCH GLOSSARY
5-st RPC Sl 2 sts to cn, hold to *back*, k3; p1, k1 from cn.
5-st LPC Sl 3 sts to cn, hold to *front*, p1, k1; k3 from cn.
6-st RC Sl 3 sts to cn, hold to *back*, k3; k3 from cn.

SEED ST (over an even number of sts)
Row 1 (RS) *K1, p1; rep from *.
Row 2 *P1, k1; rep from *. Rep rows 1 and 2 for seed st.

BAG
BAG BODY (MAKE 2)
Cast on 36 sts. Work row 2 of seed st once, then rep rows 1 and 2 once. Work chart rows 1-24 twice. Bind off in pat.

STRAP
Cast on 10 sts. Work in seed st for 60"/152.5cm. Bind off in pat.

FINISHING
Starting at center of cast-on edge on one bag body piece, sew strap along edge and up side of bag body. With opposite end of strap, sew cast-on edge to bind-off edge of strap and then sew strap to bottom and up opposite side of bag. Attach second bag body to other side of strap.

LINING
Fold fabric in half with RS facing and cut two 10" x 10½"/25.5cm x

26.5cm pieces for bag body. Cut 1 61" x 4"/155cm x 10cm piece of fabric for strap. Sew strap and lining pieces together, allowing for a ½"/1.5cm seam allowance. Attach magnetic closure, centering it to the top middle of both sides of bag. Fold under ½"/1.5cm hem along all sides of bag and press. With sewing needle and thread, sew lining into bag and strap.

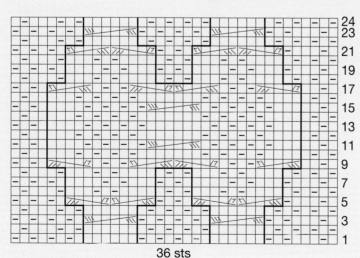

STITCH KEY
☐ K on RS, p on WS
⊟ P on RS, k on WS
▨ 5-st RPC
▨ 5-st LPC
▨ 6-st RC

36 sts

7

BOBBLE Bag

Jack Deutsch Studios

YOU'LL NEED:

YARN (6)
10½oz/300g, 150yd/120m of any bulky weight wool blend

NEEDLES
One pair size 15 (10mm) needles *or size to obtain gauge*

ADDITIONAL MATERIALS
Size E/4 (3.5mm) crochet hook
One ¾"/2cm magnetic snap
½yd/.5m of medium-weight cotton lining fabric, sewing needle and thread to match
One sheet 7 mesh plastic needlepoint canvas
3" x 7"/7.5 x 17.5cm piece of heavy-weight cardboard

MEASUREMENTS
• Approx 11"/28cm wide x 7"/18cm high (excluding handle)

GAUGE
3 bobbles to 4½"/11.5cm over bobble pat.
Take time to check gauge.

NOTE
Sides and bottom of bag are made in one piece.

STITCH GLOSSARY
p2sso Pass the 2 slipped sts over p3tog.

BOBBLE PATTERN (multiple of 2 plus 1)
Row 1 (RS) Knit.
Row 2 K1, *(p1, yo, p1, yo, p1) in next st (5 sts), k1; rep from * to end.
Row 3 Purl.
Row 4 K1, *sl 2 wyif, p3tog, p2sso, k1; rep from * to end.
Row 5 Knit.
Row 6 K2, *(p1, yo, p1, yo, p1) in next st, k1; rep from *, end k1.
Row 7 Purl.
Row 8 K2, *sl 2 wyif, p3tog, p2sso, k1; rep from *, end k1.

Rep rows 1 to 8 for bobble pat.

BAG
Cast on 17 sts. Work 4 rows in St st for top back facing. Cont in bobble pat for back, rep rows 1–8 3 times (24 rows). Cont in St st for bottom of bag and bind off 1 st at beg of next 2 rows—15 sts. Work even for 8 rows, then cast on 1 st at beg of next 2 rows—17 sts. Cont in bobble pat for front, rep rows 1–8 3 times (24 rows). Cont in St st for 4 rows for top front facing. Bind off.

HANDLE
Cast on 5 sts. Work in St st for 2 rows. Cont in bobble st until piece measures 11½"/29cm from beg, end with a WS row. Cont in St st for 2 rows. Bind off.

FINISHING
Block pieces to measurements. Sew side seams, then sew bottom edges to side edges of St st section. Fold bag facings to WS and sew in place. Sew on handle, centering each short end on side seam of bag.

LINING
To cover cardboard liner, cut two 4" x 8"/10 x 20.5cm pieces from fabric. With RS facing and using a ½"/1.3cm seam allowance, sew around three sides leaving one short edge open. Turn RS out. Insert cardboard. Fold open edge ½"/1.3cm to WS and whipstitch opening closed. Insert cardboard into bottom of bag. For lining, cut two 12" x 8½"/30.5 x 21.5cm pieces from fabric. With RS facing, sew side and bottom seams using a ½"/1.3cm seam allowance. Square bottom by folding each corner to a point. Measure 2"/5cm perpendicular to the seam line and mark this line. Sew across marked line. Fold corner points towards bottom and tack in place. Insert lining into bag. Fold top edge of lining to WS, so top edge of lining is ¼"/.6cm from base of bobbles at top edge of bag, then pin-mark for position of each side of magnetic snap. Remove lining. Install snap. Insert lining back into back, then slipstitch top edge of lining in place. For handle liner, cut a 1½" x 12"/4 x 30.5cm strip from plastic canvas. To cover strip, cut two 2½" x 13"/6.5 x 33cm pieces from fabric. Sew pieces tog as for cardboard liner. Turn RS out. Insert canvas strip. Fold open edge ½"/1.3cm to WS and whipstitch opening closed. Slipstitch long edges of handle liner to WS of handle and short edges to top edge of lining.

LADY DAY Bag

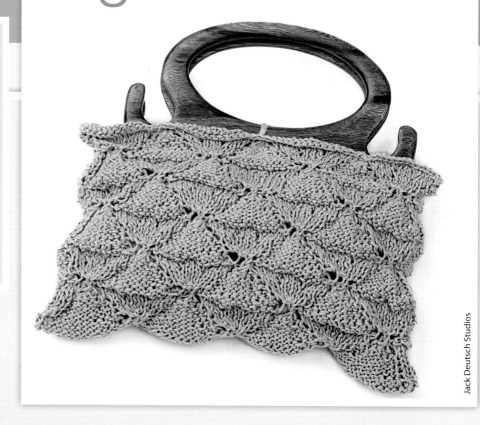

Jack Deutsch Studios

YOU'LL NEED:

YARN
7oz/200g, 380yd/350m of any worsted weight cotton

NEEDLES
One pair size 5 (3.75mm) needles *or size to obtain gauge*

ADDITIONAL MATERIALS
One pair wooden handles (www.sunbeltfashion.com)
¼yd/.25m lining fabric, sewing needle and thread to match

MEASUREMENTS
• Approx 11"/28cm wide x 7"/17.5cm high (excluding handles)

GAUGE
24 sts and 28 rows to 4"/10cm over wave pat.
Take time to check gauge.

STITCH GLOSSARY
WAVE PATTERN (multiple of 16 sts plus 3)
Row 1 (RS) K2, *p15, k1; rep from *, end p15, k2.
Row 2 P2, *k15, p1; rep from *, end k15, p2.
Row 3 K2, M1, *p2tog, p11, p2tog, M1, k1, M1; rep from *, end p2tog, p11, p2tog, M1, k2.
Row 4 P3, *k13, p3; rep from *, end k13, p3.
Row 5 K2, M1, k1, M1, *p1, [p2tog] twice, p3, [p2tog] twice, p1, M1, [k1, M1] 3 times; rep from *, end p1, [p2tog] twice, p3, [p2tog] twice, p1,[M1, k1] twice, k1.
Rows 6 and 8 P5, *k9, p7; rep from *, end k9, p5.
Row 7 K5, *p9, k7; rep from *, end p9, k5.
Row 9 K5 *[p2tog] twice, p1, [p2tog] twice, M1, k2, M1, k3, M1, k2, M1; rep from *, end [p2tog] twice, p1, [p2tog] twice, k5.
Row 10 P5, *k5 wrapping yarn around needle twice, p11; rep from *, end k5 wrapping yarn around needle twice, p5.
Row 11 K3, M1, k2, M1, *sl 5 wyib, dropping extra wrap, M1, k4, M1, k3, M1, k4, M1; rep from *, end sl 5 wyib,

dropping extra wrap, M1, k2, M1, k3.
Row 12 P7, *p5tog, p15; rep from *, end p5tog, p7.
Row 13 P5, p2tog, *M1, k1, M1, p2tog, p11, p2tog; rep from *, end M1, k1, M1, p2tog, p5.
Row 14 K6, *p3, k13; rep from *, end p3, k6.
Row 15 P1, [p2tog] twice, p1, *[M1, k1], 3 times, M1, p1, [p2tog] twice, p3, [p2tog] twice, p1; rep from *, end [M1, k1], 3 times, M1, p1, [p2tog] twice, p1.
Rows 16 and 18 K4, *p7, k9; rep from *, end p7, k4.
Row 17 P4, *k7, p9; rep from *, end k7, p4.
Row 19 P4, *M1, k2, M1, k3, M1, k2, M1, [p2tog] twice, p1, [p2tog] twice; rep from *, end M1, k2, M1, k3, M1, k2, M1, p4.
Row 20 K1, k3 wrapping yarn around needle twice, *p11, k5 wrapping yarn around needle twice; rep from *, end p11, k3 wrapping yarn around needle twice, k1.
Row 21 P1, sl 3 wyib, dropping extra wrap, *M1, k4, M1, k3, M1, k4, M1, sl 5 wyib, dropping extra wrap; rep from *, end M1, k4, M1, k3, M1, k4, M1, sl 3 wyib, dropping extra wrap, p1.
Row 22 K1, p3tog, *p15, p5tog; rep from *, end p15, p3tog, k1.

Rep rows 1 to 22 for wave pat.

BAG
BACK
Cast on 67 sts. Work in wave pat, rep rows 1 to 22 3 times; piece should measure approx 7"/18cm from beg. Bind off loosely.

FRONT
Work as for back.

FINISHING
Block pieces to measurements. Sew side and bottom seams.
LINING
Cut two 12"/30.5cm x 7"/17.5cm pieces of lining. Using a ½"/1.3cm seam allowance, sew side and bottom seams. Turn top edge ½"/1.3cm to WS and press. Insert lining. Slip stitch top edge of lining to bag. Whipstitch top edge of bag at three points to each handle as shown.

SNOWFLAKE Bag

YOU'LL NEED:

YARN 🧵 ③
3½oz/100g, 260yd/220m of any DK weight wool in blue (MC)
1¾oz/50g, 131yd/118m in ecru (CC)

NEEDLES
One pair size 6 (4mm) needles *or size to obtain gauge*

ADDITIONAL MATERIALS
Cable needle (cn)
1 set bamboo handles

MEASUREMENTS
• Approx 11½" x 10"/29cm x 25.5cm

GAUGES
One snowflake square of 27 sts by 27 rows in St st measures 4½"/11.5cm wide by 4¼"/11cm long.
20 sts and 34 rows to 4"/10cm over seed st using size 6 (4mm) needles.
Take time to check gauges.

STITCH GLOSSARY
SEED STITCH
(over an odd number of sts)
Row 1 K1, *p1, k1; rep from * to end. **Row 2** K the purl and p the knit sts.
Rep row 2 for seed st.

CABLE PATTERN (over 6 sts)
Rows 1, 3 and 7 (RS) Knit.
Rows 2, 4, 6 and 8 Purl. **Row 5** Sl 3 sts to cn and hold to back, k3, k3 from cn.

BAG
FRONT
With MC, cast on 65 sts.
Row 1 (RS) K1 (selvage st), work seed st to last st, k1 (selvage st). Cont to work selvage sts every row, work even in seed st for 3 more rows.
Beg Chart Patterns
Row 1 (RS) K1 (selvage st), work 3 sts with MC in seed st, k27 with CC foll chart 1, work 3 sts with MC in seed st, k27 with CC foll chart 2, work 3 sts with MC in seed st, k1 (selvage st). Cont to work in this way until row 27 of charts is completed.
Row 28 (WS) With MC, k1, [work 3 sts in seed st, p27] twice work 3 sts in seed st, k1. Work 3 more rows with MC in seed st. Rep row 28.
Beg Chart Patterns
Row 1 (RS) With MC k1, work 3 sts in seed st, k27 with CC foll chart 3, work 3 sts with MC in seed st, k27 with CC foll chart 4, work 3 sts with MC in seed st, k1. Cont in this way until row 27 of charts is completed. **Next row (WS)** With MC, k1 [work 3 sts in seed st, p11, p2tog, p12, p2tog] twice, work 3 sts in seed st, k1—61 sts. Work 4 more rows with MC

in seed st, dec 2 sts on last WS row—59 sts. **Next row (RS)** K1, *work 3 sts with MC in seed st, k6 with CC (for row 1 of cable pat); rep from * 5 times more, work 3 sts with MC in seed st, k1. Cont to work in this way until 8 rows of cable pat are completed.

Next row (RS) With MC, k1, M1 st, *work 3 sts in seed st, k6; rep from * 5 times more, work 3 sts with MC in seed st, M1 st, k1—61sts. Work 3 more rows in seed st. Bind off sts.

BACK

With MC, cast on 52 sts. **Row 1 (RS)** K1 (selvage st), work 50 sts in seed st, k1 (selvage st). Cont to work in this way until piece measures same as front. Bind off sts tightly.

FINISHING

Block pieces to measurements. Sew lower and side seams firmly. Place markers at 1½"/4cm from each side seam on front for casing. Pick up

and k 36 sts between markers. Work in seed st for 4 rows. Bind off. Fold casing over one handle and sew tightly in place. Work back casing in same way.

Color key

▨ Blue (MC)

☐ Ecru (CC)

CHART 1

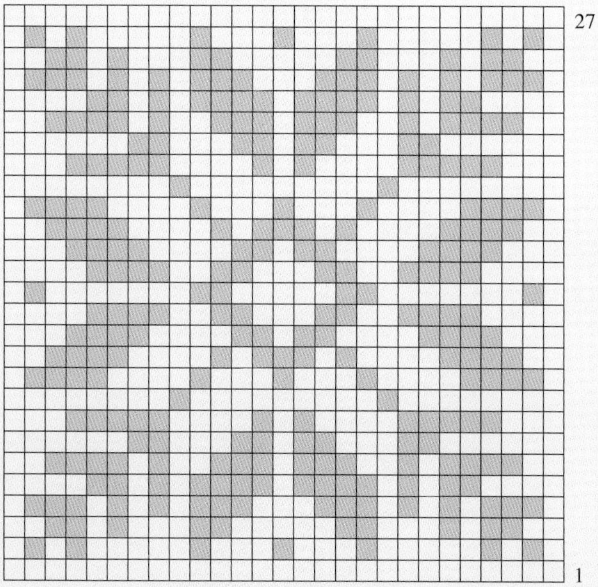

27

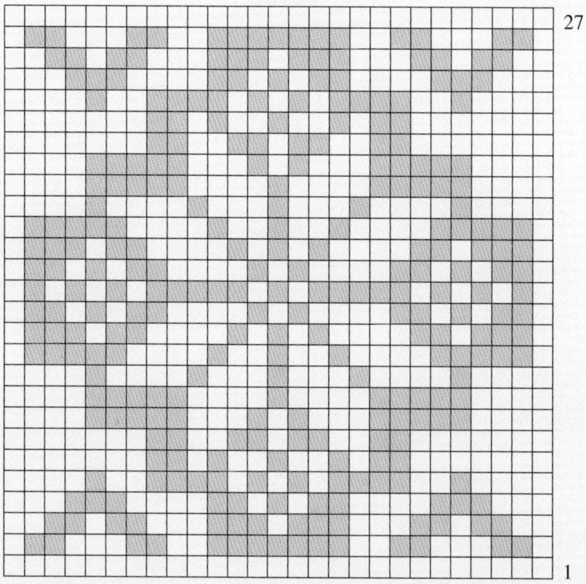

27   1

CHART 2

27

27   1

CHART 3

27

27   1

CHART 4

27

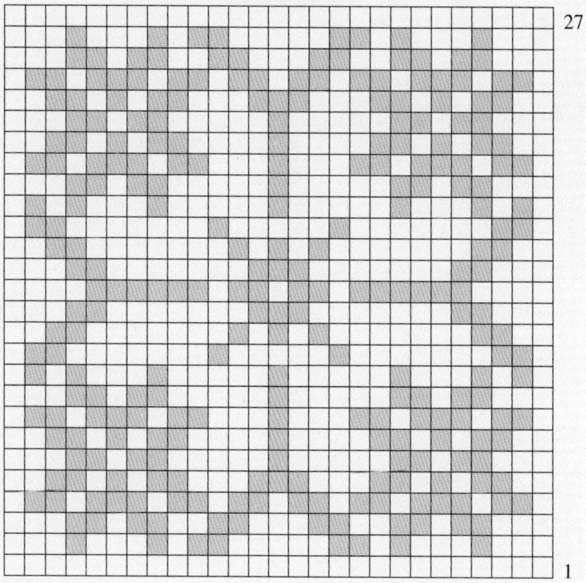

27   1

DRAWSTRING Backpack

Paul Amato for LVARepresents.com

YOU'LL NEED:

YARN (4)
7oz/200g, 340yd/315m of any worsted weight wool in teal (A)
1¾oz/50g, 85yd/70m in orange (B) and magenta (C)

NEEDLES
One size 7 (4.5mm) circular needle, 24"/60cm long *or size to obtain gauge*
One set (5) size 7 (4.5mm) double-pointed needles (dpns)

ADDITIONAL MATERIALS
One size H-8 (5mm) crochet hook
Stitch markers (one in contrasting color)
1yd/1m lining fabric
1 sheet Timtex
Sewing needle and thread
Sewing machine (optional)

MEASUREMENTS
• **Circumference** 24"/61cm
• **Height** 14"/35.5cm

GAUGE
18 sts and 24 rnds to 4"/10cm over St st in the round.
Take time to check gauge.

SPECIAL TECHNIQUE
KNITTING I-CORD WITH 2 DPNS
To knit I-cord, you'll need two double-pointed needles or one circular needle. For the cord shown, cast on 4 sts.
1 Knit one row. Do not turn.
2 Slide stitches to other end of needle to work the next row from the right side. Bringing yarn across back of work, k4.
Repeat Steps 1 and 2.

BAG
Cast on 108 sts for lower edge of bag. Place marker (of contrasting color) and join for knitting in the round taking care not to twist sts on needle.
Next rnd K27 sts, pm, k54, pm, k to rnd marker. Knit 2 rnds.
Next rnd [K to 6 sts before marker, k2tog, yo, k4, sl m, k4, yo, k2tog] twice, k to end of rnd marker.
Cont in St st until piece measures 13"/33cm from beg.

Next (eyelet) rnd K4, yo, k2tog, [k7, yo, k2tog] 11 times, k3. Work until piece measures 14"/35.5cm from beg. Bind off purlwise.

BOTTOM
Pick up and knit 108 sts along cast-on row. Place marker and join. Purl 1 rnd. Knit 2 rnds.
Next rnd *K7, k2tog; rep from * around—96 sts. K 3 rnds.
Next rnd *K6, k2tog; rep from * around—84 sts. K 3 rnds.
Next rnd *K5, k2tog; rep from * around—72 sts. K 1 rnd.
Next rnd *K4, k2tog; rep from * around—60 sts. K 1 rnd.
Next rnd *K3, k2tog; rep from * around—48 sts. K 1 rnd.
Next rnd *K2, k2tog; rep from * around—36 sts. K 1 rnd.
Next rnd *K1, k2tog; rep from * around—24 sts. K 1 rnd.
Next rnd *K2tog; rep from * around—12 sts.
Next rnd *K2tog; rep from * around—6 sts.
Cut yarn and thread through rem sts. Cinch tightly to close.

FINISHING
I-CORD STRAPS
Work two 120"/305cm I-cord straps as foll: With C, cast on 4 sts.
*Row 1 (RS) K4. Do not turn. Slide sts to beg of needle to work next row from RS. Rep from * for I-cord.
Thread cord through top of bag and thread both ends through bottom eyelets and knot together.

FLOWER
LAYER 1
With B and crochet hook, ch 6. In the 6th ch from hook, work [dc, ch 2] 7 times. Join with sl st in 3rd ch st of initial chain. (8 spokes in wheel).
Next rnd Ch 1, work [sc, ch 1, 2 dc, ch 1, sc] over each ch-2 arch. Join with sl st to first sc. Fasten off.

LAYER 2
With C, make a slip knot on hook. With WS facing, insert hook under a center spoke and work sl st to join yarn, ch 6, work [dc,

BUCKET Bag

ch 3] around each remaining spoke, sl st in 3rd ch of ch-6. (8 spokes in C).
Next rnd Ch 1, turn to RS with Layer 1 on top, work [sc, ch 1, 3 dc, ch 1, sc] over each ch-3 arch, join in first sc. Fasten off.

LAYER 3
With B, make a slip knot on hook. With WS facing, insert hook under a Layer 2 spoke and work sl st to join yarn, ch 7, work [dc, ch 4] around each remaining spoke around, sl st in 3rd ch of ch-6. (8 spokes in B).
Next rnd Ch 1, turn to RS with Layer 1 on top, work [sc, ch 1, 4 dc, ch 1, sc] over each ch-4 arch, join in first sc. Fasten off.

LAYER 4
With C, make a slip knot on hook. With WS facing, insert hook under a Layer 3 spoke and work sl st to join yarn, ch 8, work [dc, ch 5] around each remaining spoke around, sl st in 3rd ch of ch-6. (8 spokes in B).
Next rnd Ch 1, turn to RS with Layer 1 on top, work [sc, ch 1, 5 dc, ch 1, sc] over each ch-5 arch, join in first sc. Fasten off.

LAYER 5
With B, make a slip knot on hook. With WS facing, insert hook under a Layer 4 spoke and work sl st to join yarn, ch 9, work [dc, ch 6] around each remaining spoke around, sl st in 3rd ch of ch-6. (8 spokes in B).
Next rnd Ch 1, turn to RS with Layer 1 on top, work [sc, ch 1, 6 dc, ch 1, sc] over each ch-6 arch, join in first sc. Fasten off. Sew to front of bag.

LINING
Cut Timtex in a circle to fit in bottom of bag. Place in bottom of bag. Using bag for reference, cut fabric to fit bottom circle and a piece to cover side of bag. Sew side piece to bottom piece, sew up side seam. Press a ¼"/.5cm hem at top of side piece, hand sew into bag.

Paul Amato for LVARepresents.com

YOU'LL NEED:

YARN 🔵6
14oz/400g, 140yd/120m of any super-bulky wool blend

NEEDLES
One size 17 (12.75mm) circular needle, 32"/80cm long *or size to obtain gauge*
One set (5) size 17 (12.75mm) double-pointed needles (dpns)

ADDITIONAL MATERIALS
2 leather handles
¾yd/.75m lining fabric
Thread and sewing needle

MEASUREMENTS
• 9" x 5" x 12"/23cm x 12.5cm x 30.5cm

GAUGE
6½ sts and 9 rnds to 4"/10cm over St st.
Take time to check gauge.

SPECIAL TECHNIQUE
3-NEEDLE BIND-OFF
1 Hold right sides of pieces together on two needles. Insert third needle knitwise into first st of each needle, and wrap yarn knitwise.
2 Knit these two sts together, and slip

them off the needles. *Knit the next two sts together in the same manner.
3 Slip first st on 3rd needle over 2nd st and off needle. Rep from * in step 2 across row until all sts are bound off.

BAG
Cast on 46 sts, place marker and join for knitting in the round. Work in St st (knit every rnd) until piece measures 14"/35.5cm. Bind off.

BOTTOM
With RS facing and dpn, pick up 8 sts with Needle 1 around one corner, pick 15 sts with Needle 2 along side edge, 8 sts with Needle 3 around other corner, and 15 sts along other side edge with Needle 4. Attach yarn and work as foll:
Row 1 (RS) Working from Needle 1, k7, sl last st to Needle 2 and k2tog. Turn.
Row 2 (WS) P7, sl last st to Needle 4 and p2tog. Turn.
Rep rows 1 and 2 until all sts from Needles 2 and 4 needles have been worked. Work 3-needle bind-off with sts from Needle 3.

FINISHING
LINING
Cut side lining piece 29" x 13½"/73.5cm x 34.5cm. Cut bottom lining piece 9" x 5"/23cm x 12.5cm. Iron down ½"/1.5cm hem at top of side piece. Sew bottom and sides together (add pocket if desired).
Using thread and sewing needle, attach lining 1½"/4cm from top of bag. Fold knitted hem over to the inside about 2"/5cm. Secure fold with thread and sewing needle.

HANDLES
Using photo for reference, attach leather handles centered on front top on both sides with thread and needle.

13

SMALL SHOULDER Bag

Quenet Studio

■■■□

MEASUREMENTS
- **Before felting** 3¾"/9.5cm x 1¼"/3cm x 7¼"/18.5cm
- **After felting** approx 3½"/9cm x ¾"/2cm x 3¾"/9.5cm

GAUGE
11 sts and 16 rows = 4"/10cm over St st in MC, using larger needles (before felting).
Take time to check gauge.

NOTE
Bag is worked back and forth in rows for flap, then worked in rounds. Strap is worked back and forth in rows.

STITCH GLOSSARY
SSKP Slip 2 sts one at a time knitwise, knit the next st, pass the 2 sl sts over the knit st—2 sts decreased.

BAG
FLAP
With larger needles and MC, cast on 10 sts. K 2 rows.
*With 1 strand A and B held tog, k 2 rows.
With MC, k 4 rows. Rep from * twice

more. With MC, k 2 rows.

BODY
Using MC and cable cast on, cast on 18 additional sts—28 sts.
Divide sts evenly onto 2 dpns—14 sts each. Taking care not to twist sts, arrange needles so that they are parallel to each other, with the yarn hanging from the RH end of back needle. Pm on cast on row to mark beg of rnd. With third dpn, knit the first st of the front needle, pulling yarn snug to close the circle.
Rnds 1-8 With MC, knit.
Rnd 9 With B and C held tog, knit.
Rnd 10 With B and C held tog, purl.
Rnd 11 With 2 strands of A held tog, knit.
Rnd 12 With B and C held tog, knit.
Rnd 13 With B and C held tog, purl. Cut accent colors. With MC, k for 12 rnds—approx 3"/8cm.
Shape bag
Next Rnd Sskp, k8, sskp, sskp, k8, sskp—10 st rem on each needle.
Next Rnd Knit. Bind off using 3-needle bind-off.

STRAP
With circular needle and C, cast on 180 sts, using cable cast-on.
Row 1 Knit.
Rows 2 and 3 With B, knit.
Row 4 With C, bind off.

FELTING
Put items in separate zippered pillowcases/mesh bags. Set washer for low water level and hottest temperature. Add small amount of soap and items to be felted. Put through wash cycle, checking felting progress often. When desired size,

YOU'LL NEED:

YARN
4 2oz /70g, 80yd/70m of any worsted weight wool in light green (MC)
2 2oz /70g, 140yd/130m of any sport weight wool in dark orange (A)
2 2oz /70g,120yd/110m) of any variegated sport weight wool in brown multi (B)
2 2oz /70g, 120yd/110m) of any variegated sport weight wool in green multi (C)

NEEDLES
One pair size 11 (8 mm) needles *or size to obtain gauge*
One set (3) size 11 (8 mm) double-pointed needles (dpns)
Size 10 (6mm) circular needle, 24"/60cm long

ADDITIONAL MATERIALS
Tapestry needle
One ¾"/2 cm button
Stitch marker

remove from machine and rinse in cool water to remove soap and to stop felting process. Roll in dry towel to remove excess water. Shape as desired and gently stuff with a plastic bag to dry.

FINISHING
When dry, use tip of dpn to make a hole on each side of bag, just above accent stripe. Insert strap end into hole, knot strap on inside of bag to desired length. Twist 2 strands of C tog, make new strand 2"/5cm long. Knot strand, make loop and sew to bottom edge of front flap for button loop. Sew button to center front of bag, in middle of accent strip.

WASHINGTON SQUARE Bag

YOU'LL NEED:

YARN
3½oz/100g, 223yd/204m of any worsted weight wool in gold (A), chestnut brown (B), red (C), orange (D) and forest green (E)

NEEDLES
One pair size 10½ (6.5mm) needles *or size to obtain gauge*

ADDITIONAL MATERIALS
Tapestry needle

MEASUREMENTS
- **Before felting** 13½"/34cm x 19"/48cm
- **After felting** approx 10"/25.5cm x 11"/28cm

GAUGE
15 sts and 21 rows to 4"/10cm over St st (before felting).
Take time to check gauge.

BAG
SIDE 1
With A, cast on 50 sts loosely. Work in St st for 50 rows. Change to B and cont in St st for 50 more rows. Bind off loosely.

SIDE 2
With C, cast on 50 sts loosely. Work in St st for 50 rows. Change to D and cont in St st for 50 more rows. Bind off loosely.

STRAPS (make 2)
With E, cast on 5 sts loosely. Work in St st for 50"/172cm. Bind off.

FINISHING
With RS facing tog, sew side 1 and side 2 tog along side edges using mattress st and matching color changes. With RS facing tog, fold bag so that joined seams are at center of front and back of bag. Sew bottom edge closed. Weave in all ends.

FELTING
Put bag and straps in separate zippered pillowcases or mesh bags. Set washer for medium water level and hottest temperature. Add small amount of soap, a towel or pair of jeans for agitation, and items to be felted. Put through wash cycle, checking felting progress often. When desired size, remove felted item from machine and rinse in cool water to remove soap and to stop felting process. Roll in dry towel to remove excess water. Shape as desired and gently stuff with a plastic bag to dry.

STRAP HOLES
Insert knitting needle through all four layers of fold as shown in the diagram. Wiggle the needle around to open up and stretch the holes. With front side of bag facing, insert end of one strap into hole, pull through to middle of fold. Insert one end of other strap into same hole from back side of bag to middle of fold. Knot ends tog in middle of fold. Repeat on other side of bag.

Quenet Studio

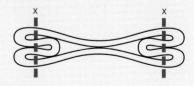

STRIPED Bag

YOU'LL NEED:

YARN ⑤
4oz/113g, 125yd/114m of any bulky weight wool in purple (A), red (B), gold (C), pink (D), blue (E), and orange (F)

NEEDLES
One pair size 10½ (6.5mm) needles *or size to obtain gauge*
Size 10½ (6.5mm) circular needle, 24"/60cm long

ADDITIONAL MATERIALS
Stitch markers
Purse handles #23900 by M&J Trimming

MEASUREMENTS
• 10 x 11"/25.5 x 28cm

GAUGE
14 sts and 28 rows to 4"/10cm over garter st.
Take time to check gauge.

STITCH GLOSSARY
STRIPE PATTERN
Work in garter st and stripe pat as foll: *2 rows A, 2 rows B, 2 rows C, 2 rows D, 2 rows E, 2 rows F; rep from * (12 rows) for stripe pat.

NOTE
When working garter st in the rnd, work k 1 rnd, p 1 rnd.

BAG
BOTTOM
With A, cast on 38 sts. Work in garter st and stripe pat until piece measures 3½"/9cm. Bind off.

SIDES
With RS facing and A, beg at corner and pick up and k12 sts along one short edge, 38 sts along one long edge, 12 sts along other short edge, 38 sts along other long edge—100 sts. Join, being careful not to twist sts. Pm at end of rnd and slip every rnd. Work in garter st and stripe pat until piece measures 10"/25.5cm from beg. Bind off.

EYE [4] MEDIA

FINISHING
Block pieces. Sew on handles to inside of front and back. Cut a piece of sturdy cardboard 3½" x 11"/9 x 28cm for bottom of bag.

CARPETBAGGER

YOU'LL NEED:

YARN 🄶
7oz/200g, 220yd/200m of any super bulky weight variegated wool

NEEDLES
One pair each sizes 9 and 10 (5.5 and 6mm) needles *or size to obtain gauge*

ADDITIONAL MATERIALS
Zipper 12"/30.5cm long

MEASUREMENTS
• Approx 12"/30.5cm wide x 10"/25.5cm high (excluding strap)

GAUGE
20 sts and 37 rows to 4"/10cm over double fabric st using larger needles.
Take time to check gauge.

STITCH GLOSSARY
S2KP Slip 2 sts knitwise, k1, pass 2 slip sts over the k1.

DOUBLE FABRIC STITCH (multiple of 4 sts)
Row 1 (RS) K1, *sl 2 wyif, k2; rep from *, end sl 2 wyif, k1.
Row 2 K1, p2, *sl 2 wyib, p2; rep from *, end k1.
Rep rows 1 and 2 for double fabric st.

BAG
BACK
Beg at top edge, with smaller needles, cast on 60 sts. K 1 row. Change to larger needles and work in double fabric st until piece measures 9"/25cm from beg, end with WS row.
Bottom shaping
Next (dec) row (RS) S2KP, *k2tog, sl 2 wyif; rep from *, end k2tog, k3tog—42 sts.
Next (bind off) row K1, sl 1 wyib, bind off, *[p1, bind off] twice, sl 1 wyib, bind off; rep from *, end k1, bind off.

FRONT
Work as for back.

GUSSET/STRAP
With larger needles, cast on 8 sts.
Row 1 (RS) K1, sl 2 wyif, k2, sl 2 wyif, k1.
Row 2 K1, p2, sl 2 wyib, p2, k1.

Jack Deutsch Studios

Rep rows 1 and 2 until piece measures 75"/190.5cm from beg. Bind off in pat st.

FINISHING
Block pieces to measurements. Sew short ends of gusset/strap tog. Center gusset/strap seam on center bottom edge of bag back. Whipstitch gusset in place. Rep on bag front. Baste zipper in place. Sew in zipper.

FELTED Sack

YOU'LL NEED:

YARN 🔵
17½oz/500g, 550yd/500m of any
bulky weight wool tweed

NEEDLES
One size 10 (6mm) circular needle,
36"/92cm long *or size to obtain gauge*
One set (4) size 10 (6mm) double-
pointed needles (dpns)

ADDITIONAL MATERIALS
4 buttons
Size I/9 (5.5mm) crochet hook
Stitch markers and holder

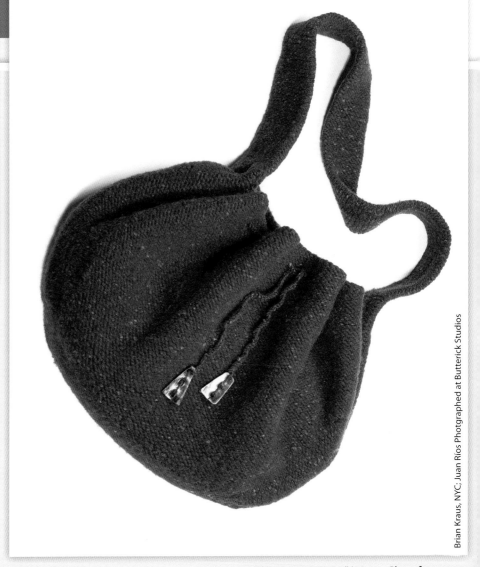

MEASUREMENTS
• **Before felting** 14"/35cm width at base,
14½"/37cm tall, strap is 39"/99cm long
by 2½"/6.5cm wide.
• **After felting** 12"/32cm width at base,
16"/40.5cm tall, strap is 35"/89cm long
by 2"/5cm wide.

GAUGE
Before felting 12 sts and 16 rows to
4"/10cm over reverse St st.
After felting 15 sts and 20 rows to
4"/10cm over reverse St st.
Take time to check gauges.

BAG
Beg at base of bag, cast on 38 sts using
provisional cast-on method as foll:
Using crochet hook and waste yarn in a
contrasting color, ch 40. With main yarn
and leaving a 10"/25.5cm tail, pick up 38
sts in back ridges of ch. Work in rev St st
(p 1 row, k 1 row) for 20 rows.

BEG RNDS
Pick up and k 20 sts along side edge of
rectangle, pm, unravel waste yarn and
pick up and k 38 sts from provisional cast-
on edge, pm, pick up and k 20 sts along
other side of rectangle, pm—116 sts. The
last marker marks beg of rnd. Join and
beg working in rnds.
Rnd 1 Sl marker, M1, p38, M1, sl marker,
p20, sl marker, M1, p38, M1, sl marker,
p20.
P 1 rnd.
Rnd 3 Inc 1 st by M1 after first marker,
M1 before 2nd marker, M1 after 3rd
marker and M1 before 4th marker. The
sts that are inc'd from the front and back
of bag and the 20 sts at each side form
the shoulder strap. Cont in reverse St st
(p every rnd), inc 4 sts as on rnd 3, every
other rnd 25 times more—220 sts. Work
even until bag measures 16"/40.5cm tall.
Bind off 90 sts, p until there are 20 sts
from bind-off and sl these sts to a holder,
bind off 90 sts.

BEG STRAP
P5 with first dpn, p10 with 2nd dpn, p5
with 3rd dpn. Join and work in rnds on
these sts (the 10 sts on 2nd dpn from
the outside of strap) in reverse St st until

strap measures 35"/89cm. Sl sts from
holder to dpn and weave tog sts from
opposite side of bag in the same order
(5, 10, 5) as strap sts. Sew open ends of
strap tog to close strap at bag top.

FINISHING
Felt bag in washing machine (add
heavy towels or old jeans for weight)
on normal cycle using hot water and a
mild detergent. Rinse in cold water. Lay
flat to dry and smooth to a neat shape.
Make two 36"/92cm ch cords leaving a
6"/15cm yarn length at each end. Work
a sl st in each ch to end. Beg at center,
pull cord through fabric, in and out at
4"/10cm intervals at 1"/2.5cm down from
bag top. Tie cords tog at center front and
back. Attach buttons to 4 cord ends.

FAIR ISLE FELTED Tote

Brian Kraus, NYC; Juan Rios Photgraphed at Butterick Studios

YOU'LL NEED:

YARN ⓷
3½oz/100g, 220yd/200m of any DK weight wool in black (A), grey (B), beige (C), and green (G)
1¾oz/50g, 110yd/100m in red (D), blue (E), and gold (F)

NEEDLES
Two size 10½ (7mm) double-pointed needles (dpns) *or size to obtain gauge*

ADDITIONAL MATERIALS
Size G/6 (4.5mm) crochet hook
One 1¼"/32mm button
26"/66cm strung wooden bead handles
Button
Stiff bristle brush (for felting)

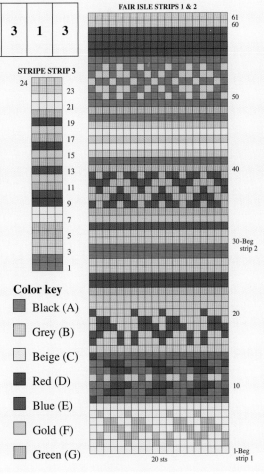

MEASUREMENTS
• 14½" x 17"/37cm x 43cm (after felting)

GAUGES
Before felting 16 sts and 17 rows to 4"/10cm in St st foll charts before felting.
After felting 18 sts and 21 rows to 4"/10cm.
Take time to check gauges.

NOTES
1 Strips are knit back and forth on 2 dpn to make changing colors at either end of row easier.
2 Bag is made with 4 alternating stripe strips and 4 Fair Isle strips and pieces are sewn tog.

BAG

FAIR ISLE STRIP 1 (make 2)
With C, cast on 20 sts. Working in St st foll chart, work rows 1-61 once then rep rows 1-24. Piece measures approx 20"/50.5cm. Bind off.

FAIR ISLE STRIP 2 (make 2)
With C, cast on 20 sts. Working in St st foll chart, work rows 30-61 once then rep rows 1-53. Bind off.

STRIPE STRIP 3 (make 4)
With A, cast on 20 sts. Working in St st foll chart, rep rows 1-24 three times, then work rows 1-13 once. Bind off.

FINISHING
Block pieces flat. Foll strip layout, assemble front and back with seams on the WS. Work a tight second seam on lower edge of bag on WS for extra strength. Do not sew side seams, but run a basting thread along top of bag to keep sts from distorting when felting.

FELTING PROCESS
Brush with stiff brush to achieve fuzzy fabric. Fold top 1"/2.5cm down to inside for hem and baste in place. Sew side seams firmly, curving lower corners. Using A, work blanket st around top edge. Using C, D and E, embroider cross sts at strip joinings foll photo. With A, make a 9"/23cm twisted cord and loop through center back and fasten in place for buttonloop. Attach handles to inside top hem at strip joinings. Sew on button.

STRIP LAYOUT

2	3	1	3

STRIPE STRIP 3

24
23
21
19
17
15
13
11
9
7
5
3
1

FAIR ISLE STRIPS 1 & 2

61
60
50
40
30-Beg strip 2
20
10
1-Beg strip 1

20 sts

Color key
- ▨ Black (A)
- ▢ Grey (B)
- ▢ Beige (C)
- ◼ Red (D)
- ▨ Blue (E)
- ▨ Gold (F)
- ▨ Green (G)

POLKA DOT Felted Bag

Paul Amato for LVARepresents.com

MEASUREMENTS
- **Before felting** 44" x 22"/112cm x 56cm
- **After felting** 32" x 14"/81.5cm x 35.5cm

GAUGE
13½ sts and 20 rows to 4"/10cm over St st (pre-felted).
Take time to check your gauge.

NOTE
Bag shrunk approximately 30% in width and 35% in height. Be sure to check your Felted measurements as yours will shrink differently depending on your washing machine and the heat of the hot and cold water.

BAG
BAG BASE
With circular needles and A, cast on 62 sts. Work in garter st 30 rows.

SIDES
Place marker, pick up 15 sts on short side of rectangle, 62 sts along cast-on row, 15 sts along short side, knit across last row of rectangle, join for knitting in the round—154 sts.
Work in garter st in the round as foll: Purl 1 rnd, knit 1 rnd.
Work for 8 rnds past pick-up row, dec'ing 4 sts evenly around on last rnd—150 sts.
Change to St st and B, work Polka Dot chart using B and C through rnd 15.
Change to A and work in St st for 13"/33cm from top of Polka Dot chart. Work Polka Dot chart using B and C through rnd 15 once more.
Change to A, [knit 1 rnd, purl 1 rnd] 5 times. Bind off.

HANDLES (make 2)
With A, cast on 98 sts. Work in garter st for 2"/5cm. Bind off.

FINISHING
FELTING
Felt pieces according to felting instructions on page 3.
Pin handles to inside of bag centering on each side with 6"/15cm between the handles. Tack approx 1"/2.5cm of handle to inside of bag.

YOU'LL NEED:

YARN (4)
10½oz/300g, 600yd/570m of any worsted weight wool in purple (A)
3½oz/100g, 200yd/180m in spring green (B)
1¾oz/50g, 100yd/85m in espresso (C)

NEEDLES
One size 10 (6mm) circular needle, 24"/60cm long *or size to obtain gauge*

ADDITIONAL MATERIALS
½yd/.5m lining fabric
Sewing needle and matching thread
Sewing machine (optional)
Stitch markers

LINING
Measure the bag and cut a piece of fabric 1"/2.5cm wider than total width of bag by about 17"/43cm long. Fold the short sides of the fabric together and pin down one side and across bottom. Using a sewing machine with matching thread, sew the seam. Turn the top open side of the lining down ½"/1.5cm and press. Pin lining into bag with wrong sides together. Using sewing thread and whipstitch, attach the lining to the inside of the bag.

POLKA DOT

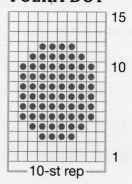

15

10

1

10-st rep

COLOR KEY
☐ Spring Green (B)
⊡ Espresso (C)

SPARKLE Clutch

Paul Amato for LVARepresents.com

MEASUREMENTS
• Approx 6" x 11"/15cm x 28cm (closed)

GAUGE
9 sts and 11 rows to 4"/10cm over garter st.
Take time to check gauge.

YOU'LL NEED:
YARN 6
7oz/200g, 240yd/220m of any super-bulky weight metallic ribbon yarn

NEEDLES
One pair size 11 (7mm) needles *or size to obtain gauge*

ADDITIONAL MATERIALS
One piece of cardboard approx 5" x 10½"/12.5cm x 26.5cm
Small amount of fabric for lining (approx ¼ yard)
Tapestry needle
One 1"/25mm button
Straight pins
Sewing needle and thread

CLUTCH
Cast on 26 sts and work in garter st (k every row) until piece measures 11"/28cm from beg.

BEG FLAP SHAPING
Next (dec) row (RS) K1, ssk, k to last 3 sts, k2tog, k1.
Purl one row.
Rep last 2 rows until 6 sts rem.
Next (buttonhole) row (RS) K2, bind off 2 sts, k2.
Next row P2, cast on 2 sts, p2.
Next (dec) row (RS) K1, ssk, k2tog, k1—4 sts.
Purl one row.
Bind off purlwise.

FINISHING
Cut length of yarn 12"/30.5cm long and sew side seams with tapestry needle.

LINING
Fold fabric in half and cut to size of clutch.
Fold edges ¼"/.5cm to WS and press.
Cut cardboard to size and place inside bag against back.
Place fabric in bag with RS facing out and fold at fold of bag. Pin fabric around top edge of clutch opening. With needle and thread, sew in place, keeping cardboard stiffener to back of clutch.
Sew button to front of clutch.

GARTER STRIPE Bag

Brian Kraus, NYC; Juan Rios Photgraphed at Butterick Studios

MEASUREMENTS
• Approx 11" x 9½"/28cm x 24cm

GAUGE
20 sts and 28 rows to 4"/10cm over garter st.
Take time to check gauge.

YOU'LL NEED:
YARN 4
3½oz/100g,320yd/290m of any worsted weight wool blend in gold (A), dk orange (B), and lt green (C)

NEEDLES
One pair size 8 (5mm) needles *or size to obtain gauge*
Two size 8 (5mm) double pointed needles (dpns)

ADDITIONAL MATERIALS
1½"/38mm toggle button

STITCH GLOSSARY
STRIPE PATTERN
Working in garter st, work 2 rows A, 2 rows B, 2 rows C. Rep these 6 rows for stripe pat.

BAG
With A, cast 38 sts. Work in stripe pat until piece measures 23"/58.5cm from beg.
Buttonhole row (RS) K17, bind off 4 sts, k to end. On next row, cast on 4 sts over bound-off sts. Cont in stripe pat until piece measures 24"/61cm from beg. Bind off.

FINISHING
Block to measurements. Fold one short end up by 10"/25.5cm. Finish side seams as folded. Flap folds over bag by 3½"/9cm.

I-CORD STRAP
With dpn and A, cast on 4 sts.
*Next row (RS) K4, do not turn. Slide sts to beg of needle to work next row from RS; rep from *until I-cord measures 46"/117cm. Bind off. Sew I-cord to outer side seams of bag, overlapping at edge by 3"/7.5cm.

DAISY Mini Tote

Brian Kraus, NYC; Juan Rios Photographed at Butterick Studios

YOU'LL NEED:

YARN (4)
3½oz/100g, 220yd/200m of any worsted weight wool in black heather (MC)
1¾oz/50g, 110yd/100m in green (A), red (B), gold (C), teal (D), orange (E) and white (F)

NEEDLES
One pair size 5 (3.75mm) needles
One set (5) size 8 (5mm) double pointed needles (dpns) *or size to obtain gauge*

ADDITIONAL MATERIALS
Tapestry needle

MEASUREMENTS
• Approx 8½" x 8"/21.5cm x 20.5cm

GAUGE
18 sts and 29 rnds to 4"/10cm over St st using larger needles. *Take time to check gauge.*

NOTE
Bag is knit in rounds using dpn. Contrast cast-on yarn is removed after knitting to graft lower edge sts tog.

BAG
Beg at lower edge with contrast (waste) yarn and dpn, cast on 80 sts. Cut waste yarn and join work, dividing sts evenly on 4 needles. With MC, k 7 rnds.
Rnd 8 *K3, work 2-st eyelet as foll: k2tog, yo twice, ssk, k3; rep from * 7 times more.
Rnd 9 K around, working into each yo as foll: p1 into the first yo, p1 tbl into the second yo.
Rnds 10-18 Knit.
Rnd 19 *Ssk, k6, k2tog, yo twice; rep from * 7 times more.
Rnd 20 Rep rnd 9.
Rnds 21-29 Knit.
Rep rnds 8-29 once more. Rep rnds 8 and 9. K 6 rnds. P 1 rnd

(for turning ridge at top). K 3 rnds. Cont in St st only, work striped lining as foll: 9 rnds A, 11 rnds B, 11 rnds C, 11 rnds D, 11 rnds E. With RS facing, divide sts evenly on 2 needles. Using E, graft sts of lining tog. Remove contrast yarn from cast-on edge and graft lower edge tog with MC. Fold lining to inside.

FINISHING
Block lightly to finished measurements. Using F, embroider daisies through both thicknesses using overcast st (see photo). Mark positions for handles at 4 rnds down from turning ridge and leaving 46 sts free at center.

HANDLES (make 2)
With contrast (waste) yarn, cast on 4 sts with size 5 (3.75mm) needles. Change to MC and work in garter st for 12½"/32cm. Leave sts on a holder. Graft straps to bag at markers.

22

CABLED Carry-All

YOU'LL NEED:

YARN ④
17½oz/500g, 1120yd/1020m of any worsted weight wool blend

NEEDLES
One pair 11 (8mm) needles *or size to obtain gauge*
One set (4) size 11 (8mm) double-pointed needles (dpns)

ADDITIONAL MATERIALS
Cable needle (cn)
One 2"/50mm novelty toggle button

MEASUREMENTS
• Approx 12" x 18"/30.5cm x 45.5cm

GAUGE
12 sts and 15 rows to 4"/10cm over St st.
Take time to check gauge.

NOTE
Work with 2 strands of yarn held tog throughout.

STITCH GLOSSARY
4-st LC Sl 2 sts to cn and hold to *front*, k2, k2 from cn.
4-st RC Sl 2 sts to cn and hold to *back*, k2, k2 from cn.
3-st LPC Sl 2 sts to cn and hold to *front*, p1, k2 from cn.
3-st RPC Sl 1 st to cn and hold to *back*, k2, p1 from cn.
8-st LC Sl 4 sts to cn and hold to *front*, k4, k4 from cn.

MAKE BOBBLE (MB)
Make 5 sts in 1 st by k1 into front, back, front, back and front of st, [turn, p5, turn k5] twice. With LH needle, pull the second, third, fourth and fifth sts one at a time over the first st and off the needle.

CABLE PATTERN (over 50 sts)
Row 1 (RS) [P2, k4] twice, p3, k2, p4, k8, p4, k2, p3, [k4, p2] twice.
Row 2 [K2, p4] twice, k3, p2, k4, p8, k4, p2, k3, [p4, k2] twice.
Row 3 [P2, 4-st LC] twice, p3, 3-st LPC, p3, k8, p3, 3-st RPC, p3, [4-st RC, p2] twice.

Row 4 [K2, p4] twice, k4, p2, k3, p8, k3, p2, k4, [p4, k2] twice.
Row 5 [P2, k4] twice, p2, MB, p1, 3-st LPC, p2, k8, p2, 3-st RPC, p1, MB, p2, [k4, p2] twice.
Row 6 [K2, p4] twice, k5, p2, k2, p8, k2, p2, k5, [p4, k2] twice.
Row 7 [P2, k4] twice, p4, 3-st RPC, p2, 8-st LC, p2, 3-st LPC, p4, [k4, p2] twice.
Row 8 Rep row 4.
Row 9 [P2, 4-st LC] twice, p3, 3-st RPC, p3, k8, p3, 3-st LPC, p3, [4-st RC, p2] twice.
Row 10 Rep row 2.
Row 11 [P2, k4] twice, p2, 3-st RPC, p1, MB, p2, k8, p2, MB, p1, 3-st LPC, p2, [k4, p2] twice.
Row 12 [K2, p4] twice, k2, p2, k5, p8, k5, p2, k2, [p4, k2] twice.
Row 13 [P2, k4] twice, p2, 3-st LPC, p4, k8, p4, 3-st RPC, p2, [k4, p2] twice.
Rep rows 2-13 for cable pat.

BAG
FRONT
With 2 strands of yarn, beg at top edge, cast on 42 sts.
Row 1 (RS) K2, *p2, k2; rep from * to end.
Row 2 P2, *k2, p2; rep from * to end. Rep row 1 once more.
Preparation row (WS) [K2, p2, p into front and back of next st for inc 1-p] twice, k3, inc 1-p, k4, inc 1-p, p4, inc 1-p, k4, inc 1-p, k3, [p2, inc 1-p, k2] twice—50 sts.

Beg cable pat
Work rows 1-13 once, omitting bobbles on rows 5 and 11 (work p1 instead, this is so that bobbles are not protruding when flap is closed), then rep rows 2-13 twice more. Bind off knitwise.

BACK AND FLAP
With 2 strands of yarn, cast on 50 sts. Work rows 1-13 of cable pat, then rep rows 2-13 three times more.
Beg flap
Next row (WS) P2tog, work pat to last 2 sts, p2tog.
Next row (RS) SKP, work pat to last 2 sts, k2tog. Rep these 2 rows 11 times more—

2 sts rem. Cut yarn and draw through sts tightly.

STRAP AND GUSSET
Cast on 20 sts.
Rows 1, 3, 5 (RS) P6, k8, p6.
Row 2 and all WS rows K6, p8, k6.
Row 7 P6, 8-st LC, p6.
Rows 9 and 11 P6, k8, p6.
Row 12 K6, p8, k6.
Rep rows 1-12 for 21 times more. Strap measures approx 76"/193cm. Bind off.

FINISHING
Block pieces to measurements. Sew long sides of strap tog forming a tube. Sew cast-on and bound-off edges tog. With cabled edge of strap to outside and center short seam on bottom of bag, sew to outside edges of bag, joining back and front tog for bottom and side gussets. Sew upper (extended) edge of back to inside of strap (to anchor strap in place.)

I-CORD TRIM
With 2 strands of yarn and with dpn, cast on 4 sts.
***Next row (RS)** K4, do not turn. Slide sts to beg of needle to work next row from RS; rep from * until I-cord fits along triangular edge of flap plus 2"/5cm extra for buttonloop. Bind off.
Pin I-cord to edge of flap and sew in place leaving the 2"/5cm free at point for buttonloop. Sew button opposite buttonloop.

FELTED Watermelon Tote

Jack Deutsch Studios

YOU'LL NEED:

YARN (4)
4oz/113g, 200yd/175m of any worsted weight wool in dk green (A), bright green (B), and bright pink (C)

NEEDLES
One set (4) size 10½ (6.5mm) double-pointed needles (dpns) *or size to obtain gauge*

ADDITIONAL MATERIALS
Stitch holders and markers

MEASUREMENTS
• Approx 8½"/21.5cm wide x 9"/23cm high (excluding handles)

GAUGE
16 sts and 20 rnds to 4"/10cm over St st (before felting).
Take time to check gauge.

NOTE
Bag is worked in the round from the bottom up.

BAG
With A, cast on 9 sts. Divide sts evenly between 3 needles with 3 sts on each needle. Join, taking care not to twist sts on needle. Pm for beg of rnd and sl marker every rnd. K next rnd.
Next (inc) rnd *K1, inc 1 in next st; rep from *, end k1—13 sts. K next rnd.
Next (inc) rnd *Inc 1 in each st around—26 sts. K next 2 rnds.
Next (inc) rnd *K1, inc 1 in next st; rep from * around—39 sts. K next 3 rnds.
Next (inc) rnd *K2, inc 1 in next st; rep from * around—52 sts. K next 4 rnds.
Next (inc) rnd *K2, inc 1 in next st; rep from *, end k1—69 sts. K next 4 rnds.
Next (inc) rnd *K2, inc 1 in next st; rep from * around—92 sts. K next 5 rnds.
Next (dec) rnd *K13, k2tog; rep from *, end k2—86 sts. K next 15 rnds.

BEG STRIPE PATTERN
Change to B and k next 3 rnds. Change to C and k next 45 rnds. Change to B and k next 2 rnds.
Next rnd [K5 sts, place on holder for strap, bind off 25 sts, k5 place on holder for strap, bind off 8 sts] twice.

HANDLE
With RS facing and B, sl 5 sts from a st holder to dpn. Work in I-cord as foll: ***Next row (RS)** With 2nd dpn, k5, do not turn. Slide sts back to beg of needle to work next row from RS; rep from * until I-cord measures 12"/30.5cm. Cut yarn. Join I-cord to 5 sts on holder on same side of bag using Kitchener stitch or 3-needle bind-off. Rep for opposite side of bag for second handle.

FINISHING
FELTING
Place piece in a zippered pillowcase and put into washing machine. Use hot-water wash and a regular (not delicate) cycle. Add a tablespoon of laundry detergent and an old pair of jeans for agitation. Check the piece frequently, agitating until stitches are not seen. Rinse in cold water and remove piece from pillowcase. Shape bag to finished measurements, then allow to air dry. Shape bag by placing a 4–5"/10–12.5cm diameter plate, lid, or bowl in bottom of bag and stretching gently into shape. Allow to dry completely.

CABLED Backpack

p1 and k1 in next yo; rep from * once, rib to end. Work even until rib measures 4"/10cm. Bind off in rib.

I-CORD
With dpn, cast on 2 sts. *Next row (RS) K2, do not turn. Slide sts to beg of needle to work next row from RS; rep from * until I-cord measures 50"/127cm. Bind off.

FINISHING
Block to measurements. Fold bag in half and sew side seams leaving 2 sts free for side gussets. Fold over rib trim at top and sew in place. Pull I-cord through eyelet opening and knot once at back. Pull one end through side gusset at left bottom edge and knot, then at right bottom edge and knot.

YOU'LL NEED:

YARN (4)
10½oz/300g, 660yd/610m of any worsted weight wool tweed

NEEDLES
One pair each sizes 5 and 7 (3.75 and 4.5mm) needles
or size to obtain gauge
Two size 5 (3.75mm) double-pointed needles (dpns)

ADDITIONAL MATERIALS
Cable needle (cn)

MEASUREMENTS
• Approx 13½" x 13"/34cm x 33cm

GAUGE
23 sts and 27 rows to 4"/10cm over cable pat using larger needles.
Take time to check gauge.

STITCH GLOSSARY
4-st RC Sl 2 sts to cn and hold to *back*, k2, k2 from cn.

4-st LC Sl 2 sts to cn and hold to *front*, k2, k2 from cn.

4-st RPC Sl 2 sts to cn and hold to *back*, k2, p2 from cn.

4-st LPC Sl 2 sts to cn and hold to *front*, p2, k2 from cn.

MAKE BOBBLE K into the front, back, front, back and front of st to make 5 sts, sl these 5 sts to LH needle, [k5, sl these 5 sts back to LH needle] twice, k3tog, ssk, psso.

BAG
With smaller needles, beg at top edge, cast on 76 sts. Work in k1, p1 rib for 4"/10cm, end with a RS row. Change to larger needles and p 1 row.
Beg chart pat
Row 1 (RS) Beg as indicated, work 12-st rep 6 times, end as indicated. Cont to foll chart in this way, rep rows 1-44 three times, rows 1-25 once. Change to smaller needles and p next row. Work in k1, p1 rib for 1"/2.5cm.
Eyelet row (RS) Work 29 sts, k2tog, yo, ssk, work 10 sts, k2tog, yo, ssk, work to end.
Next row *Work rib to eyelet,

Stitch key
- ☐ K on RS, p on WS
- ☐ P on RS, k on WS
- 4-st RC
- 4-st RPC
- 4-st LC
- 4-st LPC
- ● MB

44 43 41 39 37 35 33 31 29 27 25 23 21 19 17 15 13 11 9 7 5 3 1

end   12-st rep   beg

ROSEBUD LACE Travel Bag

Brian Kraus, NYC; Juan Rios
Photgraphed at Butterick Studios

YOU'LL NEED:

YARN

3½oz/100g, 380yd/340m of any fingering weight cotton in violet (MC)
1¾oz/50g, 187yd/170m in magenta (A), dk teal (B), bright pink (C), black (D), lt pink (E), and cream (F)

NEEDLES

One pair each sizes 2 and 4 (2.5 and 3.5mm) needles *or size to obtain gauge*
One set (5) size 4 (3.5mm) double-pointed needles (dpns)

ADDITIONAL MATERIALS

Size 5 steel (1.75mm) crochet hook
1 pkg dk blue bugle beads
1 pkg mother-of-pearl small round beads
7¾"/19.5cm diameter cardboard circle
½yd/.5m silk for lining

MEASUREMENTS

• Approx 10" x 8"/25.5cm x 20.5cm

GAUGE

24 sts and 32 rows to 4"/10 cm over body pat st using larger needles.
Take time to check gauge.

STITCH GLOSSARY

LITTLE VINE PATTERN (over 10 sts)
Row 1 (RS) K4, yo, k1, ssk, k3. **Row 2** P2, p2tog tbl, p1, yo, p5. **Row 3** K6, yo, k1, ssk, k1. **Row 4** P2tog tbl, p1, yo, p7. **Row 5** K3, k2tog, k1, yo, k4. **Row 6** P5, yo, p1, p2tog, p2. **Row 7** K1, k2tog, k1, yo, k6.
Row 8 P7, yo, p1, p2tog.
Rep rows 1-8 for little vine pat.

BAG

BASE

With dpn and MC, cast on 8 sts. Join and divide sts onto 4 dpn.
Rnd 1 [Yo, k1] 8 times. **Rnd 2** [Yo, k2tog] 8 times. **Rnd 3** [Yo, k2] 8 times. **Rnd 4** [Yo, k1, k2tog] 8 times. **Rnd 5** [Yo, k3] 8 times. **Rnd 6** [Yo, k2, k2tog] 8 times.
Rnd 7 [Yo, k4] 8 times. **Rnd 8** [Yo, k3, k2tog] 8 times. **Rnd 9** [Yo, k5] 8 times.
Rnd 10 [Yo, k4, k2tog] 8 times. **Rnd 11** [Yo, k6] 8 times. **Rnd 12** [Yo, k5, k2tog] 8 times.
Rnd 13 [Yo, k7] 8 times. **Rnd 14** [Yo, k6, k2tog] 8 times. **Rnd 15** [Yo, k8] 8 times.
Rnd 16 [Yo, k7, k2tog] 8 times.
Rnd 17 [Yo, k9] 8 times. **Rnd 18** [Yo, k8, k2tog] 8 times. **Rnd 19** [Yo, k10] 8 times.
Rnd 20 [Yo, k9, k2tog] 8 times. **Rnd 21** [Yo, k11] 8 times. **Rnd 22** [Yo, k10, k2tog] 8 times. **Rnd 23** [Yo, k12] 8 times.
Rnd 24 [Yo, k11, k2tog] 8 times. **Rnd 25** [Yo, k13] 8 times. **Rnd 26** [Yo, k12, k2tog] 8 times. **Rnd 27** [Yo, k14] 8 times.
Rnd 28 [Yo, k13, k2tog] 8 times. **Rnd 29** [Yo, k15] 8 times. **Rnd 30** [Yo, k14, k2tog] 8 times. **Rnd 31** [Yo, k16] 8 times.
Rnd 32 [Yo, k15, k2tog] 8 times. **Rnd 33** [Yo, k17] 8 times. **Rnd 34** [Yo, k16, k2tog] 8 times. **Rnd 35** [Yo, k18] 8 times.
Rnd 36 [Yo, k16, k2tog] 8 times.

Color key

- ▨ Violet (MC)
- ▨ Magenta (A)
- ▨ Dark Teal (B)
- ▨ Bright Pink (C)
- ■ Purple (D)
- ▢ Light pink (E)
- ▢ Cream (F)

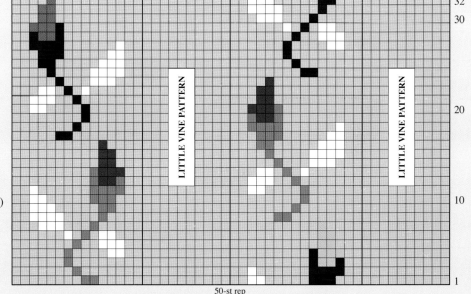

LITTLE VINE PATTERN

LITTLE VINE PATTERN

50-st rep

Circumference of circle measures approx 26"/66cm. Bind off.

BAG SIDES

With smaller needles and A, cast on 150 sts. K 2 rows A, 2 rows B, 2 rows C, 2 rows D and 2 rows A. Change to larger needles.

Beg chart pat

Row 1 (RS) Work 50-st rep 3 times. Cont to foll chart through row 32. Then rep rows 1-32 once more. With MC, k 1 row, p 1 row. **Next (eyelet) row** *K4, yo, k2tog; rep from * to end. [P 1 row, k 1 row] twice. **Next row (WS of pat)** Beg with row 1, work little vine pat over all 150 sts. (Thus, WS and RS of pat are reversed for bag drawstring top). Cont in this way until 16 rows of pat have been worked. Change to smaller needles. K 2 rows D, 2 rows A. Bind off.

FINISHING

Block pieces to measurements. Sew side seam of bag. Sew bag sides to base.

PICOT EDGE

Beg at top edge seam, with crochet hook and A, join and ch 3, sl st in same st with joining, *work sl st in next 3 sts, ch 3, sl st in last sl st worked; rep from * around. Work picot edge in same way into the A rnd at bottom of bag and base joining.

BEADING

Along picot edge, with matching sewing thread, sew 3 pearl beads in each picot and one bugle bead into 3 sl st space.

LINING

Cover cardboard circle with lining. Cut a 10" x 27"/25.5cm x 68.5cm length of fabric for lining. Sew lining to base. Tack top of lining to bag just below eyelet row. Make a 42"/107cm twisted cord with colors A, B, C, D and E. Knot ends and cover knot with a circle of bugle beads trimmed at top and bottom with pearls.

YOU'LL NEED:

YARN (4)
4oz/120g, 240yd/210m of any worsted weight wool in black (MC)
2oz/60g, 120yd/108m in red(CC)

NEEDLES
One set (4) size 10½ (7mm) double-pointed needles (dpns) *or size to obtain gauge*

ADDITIONAL MATERIALS
One 2 ¼"/60mm novelty hand button

MEASUREMENTS
• Approx 8" x 6"/20.5cm x 15cm (after felting)

GAUGE
12 sts and 20 rnds to 4"/10cm over St st.
Take time to check gauge.

NOTE
Bag is knit in rnds on dpns beg at top edge and ending at lower rounded edge. Flap sts are picked up and knit after bag is worked.

BAG
Beg at top edge, cast on 40 sts. Divide sts evenly on 3 needles. Join, taking care not to twist sts on needle. Mark end of rnd and sl marker every rnd. Work in rnds of St st for 31 rnds.
Dec rnd 1 Ssk, k2tog, k16, ssk, k2tog, k16—36 sts. K 1 rnd.
Dec rnd 2 Ssk, k2tog, k14, ssk, k2tog, k14—32 sts. K 1 rnd.
Dec rnd 3 Ssk, k2tog, k12, ssk, k2tog, k12—28 sts.
Cont to dec 4 sts in this way every rnd, having 2 less sts between double decs, until 6 sts rem. Pull yarn through rem sts and fasten off.

FLAP
Pick up and k 20 sts along one side of cast-on edge so that seam is on

inside of bag. Working back and forth in rows with 2 dpn, work in St st for 19 rows.

Top shaping
Dec row 1 (RS) Ssk, k16, k2tog—18 sts. P 1 row, k 1 row.
Dec row 2 P2tog, p14, p2tog—16 sts. K 1 row, p 1 row.
Dec row 3 Ssk, k1, ssk, k1, ssk, k2tog, k1, k2tog, k1, k2tog—10 sts. P 1 row.
Dec row 4 [Ssk] twice, k2, [k2tog] twice. Bind off rem 6 sts.

FINISHING
Refer to page 24 for information on felting. Lay bag flat to dry. Trim fuzz if desired.

BRAIDED CORD
Using 3 strands of MC for each section, make a 50"/127cm length braid to attach around outer contours of bag and to form strap. Knot at end and leave ends for tassel. With CC, embroider French knots through center of cord at ½"/1.25cm intervals for the 18"/45.5cm that cord fits to contour of bag. Sew cord in place and knot firmly at tassel end. Attach novelty hand button to flap. Make a 2"/5cm braided strip for closure for hand button. Attach to bag firmly for button and trim ends.

Brian Kraus, NYC; Juan Rios Photgraphed at Butterick Studios

CHAIN LINK Backpack

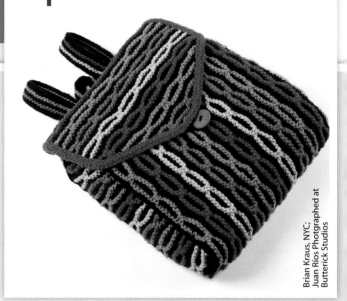

Brian Kraus, NYC;
Juan Rios Photgraphed at
Butterick Studios

YOU'LL NEED:

YARN (4)
3½oz/100g, 280yd/250m of any worsted weight wool in black (MC)

1¾oz/50g, 140yd/125m in gold (A), pink (B), teal (C) and orange (D)

NEEDLES
One pair size 7 (4.5mm) needles *or size to obtain gauge*
One each sizes 5 and 7 (3.75 and 4.5mm) circular needle, 16"/42cm long
Two size 7 (4.5mm) double-pointed needles (dpns)

ADDITIONAL MATERIALS
Three 1"/25mm buttons

MEASUREMENTS
• Approx 12"/30.5cm square

GAUGE
21 sts and 36 rows to 4"/10cm over chain link pat st using larger needles.
Take time to check gauge.

STITCH GLOSSARY
CHAIN LINK PATTERN
(multiple of 8 sts plus 6)
Row 1 (RS) With MC, knit.
Row 2 With MC, purl.
Rows 3 and 4 With A, knit.
Row 5 With MC, k6, *sl 2 wyib, k6; rep from * to end.
Row 6 With MC, p6, *sl 2 wyif, p6; rep from * to end.
Row 7 With A, rep row 5.
Row 8 With A, knit.
Rows 9 and 10 With MC, rep rows 1 and 2.
Rows 11 and 12 With B, knit.
Row 13 With MC, k2, *sl 2 wyib, k6; rep from *, end sl 2 wyib, k2.
Row 14 With MC, p2, *sl 2 wyif, p6; rep from *, end sl 2 wyif, p2.
Row 15 With B, rep row 13.
Row 16 With B, knit.
Rows 17-32 Rep rows 1-16, substituting C for A and D for B.
Rep rows 1-32 for chain link pat.

BAG
MAIN SECTION
With MC cast on 118 sts. Work in chain link pat until piece measures 10"/25.5cm, ending with third C stripe and 2 rows with MC. Bind off. Along cast-on and bound-off rows, mark center 3"/7.5cm and place yarn markers each side of center.

SIDE GUSSETS
Along one edge from RS, with MC, pick up and k 16 sts between markers. P 1 row. Beg with pat row 3, work in chain link pat for 3½"/9cm. Dec 1 st each side of next RS row—14 sts. Cont in pat until piece measures 7"/18cm. Dec 1 st each side of next RS row—12 sts. Work even until piece measures 9½"/24cm and piece fits along side edge of bag, end with a WS row in MC. Bind off.
Work other side gusset between markers on other edge in same way. Block pieces lightly. Sew gussets to main section with MC so that seam shows on RS.

TOP RIBBING
With RS facing, smaller circular needle and B, pick up and k 132 sts around top opening of bag. Join and mark beg of rnd. Work in k2, p2 rib for ½"/1.25cm.
Eyelet rnd *K2, yo, p2tog, k2, p2; rep from * around.
Work even until rib measures 1"/2.5cm. With MC, rib 1 rnd, then bind off in rib.

FLAP
With RS of back of bag facing and MC, pick up and k 46 sts evenly along back edge. P 1 row on WS. Beg with pat row 3, work in chain link pat for 5¼"/13.5cm. Bind off 2 sts at beg of next 20 rows. Bind off rem 6 sts.
Flap trim
With RS facing, smaller circular needle and B, pick up and k 110 sts around entire flap edge. Change to larger circular needle and k 1 row, p 1 row. Bind off knitwise on WS.

BACK STRAPS
With MC, cast on 100 sts. K 1 row. With C, k 2 rows. With MC, k 2 rows forming a 4-st buttonhole (bind off 4 sts, then cast on 4 sts over bound-off sts on foll row) at 4 sts from one end. With D, k 2 rows. With MC, k 1 row and bind off. Work a second back strap substituting B for C and A for D.

BACK LOOP
With MC, cast on 20 sts. K 1 row. With C, k 2 rows. With MC, k 1 row. Bind off. Sew back loop to center back. Sew straps either side of back loop, then sew buttonhole ends to lower side gussets. Sew on a button to back opposite each strap buttonhole.

I-CORD DRAWSTRING
With 2 dpn and MC, cast on 3 sts.
***Next row** K3, do not turn. Slide sts to beg of needle to work next row from RS; rep from * until I-cord measures 36"/91.5cm. Bind off. Pull drawstring through eyelets in rib. Make a 2"/5cm I-cord for buttonloop on flap. Sew to flap. Sew on button to front opposite loop.

PAISLEY Carry-All Carpetbag

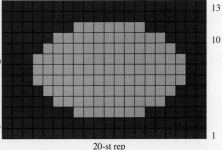

Brian Kraus, NYC; Juan Rios
Photographed at Butterick Studios

YOU'LL NEED:

YARN (4)

10½oz/300g, 570yd/530m of any worsted weight wool blend in dark grey (A) and marigold (B)

3½oz/100g, 200yd/180m in navy (C), green (D), couscous (E), and raspberry (F)

NEEDLES

Size 6 (4mm) circular needle, 32"/80cm long *or size to obtain gauge*

ADDITIONAL MATERIALS

Bobbins
Stitch marker
1¾yd/1.6m of webbing for handles
²/₃ yd/.6m buckram
½yd/.5m lining fabric

MEASUREMENTS

• Approx 40" x 46"/101.5cm x 117cm

GAUGE

21 sts and 23 rows to 4"/10 cm over paisley chart.
Take time to check gauge.

NOTES

1 When changing colors, twist yarns on WS to prevent holes in work. Carry color not in use loosely across WS.
2 Paisley motifs are worked with A. Contrasting colors are worked in duplicate st and French knots in desired colors (see photo and chart for inspiration.)

BAG

With C, cast on 126 sts. Join, taking care not to twist sts. Mark end of rnd and sl marker every rnd. P 2 rnds. Change to B and k 1 rnd, inc 14 sts evenly around—140 sts.

BEG PAISLEY CHART

Rnd 1 Work 14-st rep 10 times. Cont in this way through rnd 33, then rep rnds 2-33 once more. Work 2 rnds St st with B. Change

to F and k 1 rnd, p 2 rnds.

BEG OVAL CHART

Rnd 1 Work 20-st rep 7 times. Cont in this way through rnd 13. With F, k 1 rnd, p 2 rnds. Bind off knitwise.

EMBROIDERY

With D, E and F, duplicate st center of paisley motif in desired colors. Then embroider French knots in center of paisleys using B, C, E, and F.

HANDLES (make 2)

With F, cast on 10 sts. Working back and forth in rows, work in garter st for 30"/76cm. Bind off.

BASE

With A cast on 50 sts. Work in rev St st as foll: 4 rows each A, D, F, C, B and A. Bind off knitwise in A.
Sew base around bottom of bag.

FINISHING

Using ¾"/20mm webbing for handles, stitch handle around webbing. Attach to bag at opposite sides.

Cut a piece of buckram to fit around inside of bag. Baste in place. Cut a smaller piece for the base of bag and baste in place.
Cut a piece of lining fabric enough to go around inside of bag with a 1"/2.5cm seam down 1 side and across the bottom. Sew. Turn down top edge and sew to inside of bag.
Trace bottom of bag and cut a piece of cardboard to reinforce bottom. Cut a piece of lining fabric to cover it and glue in place. Place the cardboard piece in bottom of bag and remove when laundering.

Color key

■	Grey (A)
▨	Marigold (B)
■	Navy (C)
▨	Green (D)
□	Couscous (E)
■	Raspberry (F)
V	Duplicate stitch

PAISLEY CHART

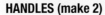

14-st rep

OVAL CHART

20-st rep

PAILLETTE Bag

Jack Deutsch Studios

MEASUREMENTS
• Approx 11"/28cm wide x 8½"/21.5cm high x 2"/5cm deep (excluding strap)

GAUGE
18 sts and 24 rnds to 4"/10cm over St st using larger needle.
Take time to check gauge.

NOTES
1 Each half of bottom of bag is worked back and forth on circular needle.
2 Body of bag is worked in the round.
3 Each row on chart is work from right to left.
4 To add a shell button or paillette, insert crochet hook into hole of button (or paillette). Use hook to remove st from LH needle, then draw this st through hole. Use hook to place st back on LH needle, then knit the st in the usual manner.

BAG
BOTTOM
With circular needle, cast on 39 sts. Work back and forth in garter st for 10 rows; place sts on holder. With circular needle, cast on another 39 sts. Work back and forth in garter st for 10 rows.

Next rnd K 39 sts from holder, cast on 9 sts, k next 39 sts on needle, then cast on 9 sts—96 sts. Pm for beg rnds.

BODY
Beg with a p rnd, work around in garter st for 8 rnds. Knit next 2 rnds.

Beg chart pat
Rnd 1 Work 12-st rep 6 times adding shell buttons (or paillettes) as described in note. Cont in this manner through rnd 39. Knit next rnd.

Divide for strap
Next rnd K33, k15 and place sts on holder for strap, k33, k15 and place sts on holder for strap.

Top edging
Next 2 rows *P33 turn, wyif, sl next st, turn; rep from * once more. Bind off sts knitwise. Rep for other side of bag.

First half of strap
Slip 15 sts from holder to smaller dpn. Purl next row.

Next (dec) row (RS) K 1, ssk, k to last 3 sts, k2tog, k1. Work next 3 rows even. Rep last 4 rows 3 times more—7 sts. Change to larger dpn and work I-cord over these 7 sts as foll: *Next row (RS) With 2nd dpn, k7, do not turn. Slide sts back to beg of needle to work next row from RS; rep from * until I-cord measures 16"/ 40.5cm. Place sts on holder.

Second half of strap
Work as for first half. Weave sts tog using Kitchener st.

FINISHING
Sew center and corner seams on bottom of bag. Thread ribbon through I-cord strap. Making sure ribbon is centered side to side, turn cut ends of ribbon to WS and sew in place. Sew side edges of ribbon to WS of strap to beg of I-cord rows.

I-CORD TIES (make 2)
With smaller dpn, cast on 3 sts. Work I-cord over these 3 sts as foll:
*Next row (RS) With 2nd dpn, k3, do not turn. Slide sts back to beg of needle to work next row from RS; rep from * until I-cord measures 12"/30.5cm. Cut yarn leaving a long tail. Thread tail in tapestry needle and weave through sts. Pull tight to gather, fasten securely, then sew a shell button (or paillette) to end of I-cord. Sew other end to center top edge of bag.

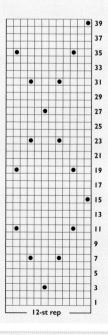

Color Key
☐ Knit
◉ Add Shell button (or paillette)

|—— 12-st rep ——|

MARKET Bag

Jack Deutsch Studios

YOU'LL NEED:

YARN
7oz/200g, 380yd/350m of
any worsted weight cotton in
champagne (MC)
3½oz/100g, 190yd/175m in coral (CC)

NEEDLES
Size 11 (8mm) circular needle,
24"/60cm long *or size to obtain gauge*
One pair size 9 (5.5mm) needles

ADDITIONAL MATERIALS
Size I/9 (5.5mm) crochet hook
Stitch marker
Four large wooden beads (optional)

MEASUREMENTS
• Approx 18"/46cm wide x 14"/35.5cm
high (excluding handles)

GAUGE
12 sts and 14 rnds to 4"/10cm over St st
using using 2 strands of yarn and larger needle.
Take time to check gauge.

NOTES
1 Use 2 strands of yarn held tog throughout.
2 Bag is made in one piece
3 Each handle/strap is made separately.

STITCH GLOSSARY
EYELET PATTERN
Rnd 1 K1, *k2tog, yo twice, ssk, k2; rep from *, end last rep k1.
Rnd 2 K2, *work (k1, p1 in double yo), k4; rep from *, end last rep k2.
Rnd 3 Yo, ssk, *k2, k2tog, yo twice, ssk; rep from *, end last rep k2tog, yo.
Rnd 4 P1 in yo, k4, *work (k1, p1 in double yo), k4; rep from *, end last rep k1 in yo.
Rep rnds 1–4 for eyelet pat.

BAG
With circular needle and 1 strand MC and CC held tog, cast on 90 sts. Join, taking care not to twist sts on needle. Pm for beg of rnd. Work around in garter st for 22 rnds. Knit next rnd. Cont in eyelet pat, rep rows 1–4 3 times.
Change to 2 strands of MC. Cont in eyelet pat, rep rows 1–4 3 times. Change to 2 strands of CC.

Cont in eyelet pat, rep rows 1–4 twice.

HANDLE/STRAP (make 2)
With smaller needles and 2 strands of MC held tog, cast on 4 sts. Work in garter st for 48"/122cm. Bind off.

FINISHING
Block pieces to measurements. Sew bottom edges of bag tog. Sew short edges of each handle/strap tog. Place bag flat on work surface. Position first handle/strap around bag, matching seams and so outer side edge of handle/strap is 3"/8cm from side edge of bag. Pin in place beg at bottom edge to beg of CC eyelet rnds. Using one strand of CC, whipstitch side edges of handle/strap in place. Rep for rem handle/strap.

DRAWSTRING
With crochet hook and 1 strand of MC and CC held tog, ch 48"/122cm. Beg and ending at center front, weave drawstring through eyelets of next to last row. Thread beads onto drawstring ends, then knit ends to secure.

FELTED DIAMOND Bag

MEASUREMENTS
• Approx 10½"/26.5 wide x 9¼"/23.5 high (excluding straps)

GAUGE
One square to 2½"/6.5cm (before felting).
Take time to check gauge.

BAG
SQUARE 1
With MC, cast on 10 sts. K 20 rows, do not cut yarn.
SQUARE 2
*With same MC, cast on 10 sts using cable cast-on. K 20 rows, do not cut yarn; rep from * twice more for squares 3 and 4—40 sts on needle.
SQUARE 5
Sl 10 sts of square 4 to RH needle. With E, pick up and k 10 sts along left side of square 4. *Turn and k10, turn, k9, k last st tog with first st of square 3; rep from * until no sts of square 3 rem. Cut yarn.
SQUARE 6
With A, pick up and k 10 sts along left side of square 3. *Turn and k10, turn, k9, k last st tog with first st of square 3; rep from * until no sts of square 3 rem. Cut yarn.

SQUARE 7
With E, pick up and k 10 sts along left side of square 2. *Turn and k10, turn, k9, k last st tog with first st of square 1; rep from * until no sts of square 1 rem. Cut yarn.
SQUARE 8
Turn piece so that square 1 is on the right and square 4 is on the left. With a spare

needle, pick up and k 10 sts from the cast-on row of square 2. With E, pick up and k 10 sts along right side of square 1. *Turn and k10, turn, k9, k last st tog with first st of square 2; rep from * until no sts of square 2 rem. Cut yarn.
SQUARE 9
With a spare needle, pick up and k 10 sts from the cast-on row of square 3. With A,

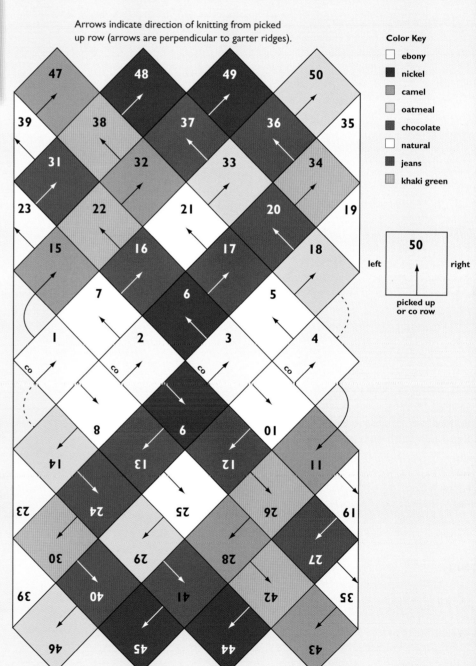

Arrows indicate direction of knitting from picked up row (arrows are perpendicular to garter ridges).

Color Key
□ ebony
■ nickel
■ camel
□ oatmeal
■ chocolate
□ natural
■ jeans
■ khaki green

pick up and k 10 sts along right side of square 2. *Turn and k10, turn, k9, k last st tog with first st of square 3; rep from * until no sts of square 3 rem. Cut yarn.

SQUARE 10
With a spare needle, pick up and k 10 sts from the cast-on row of square 4. With E, pick up and k 10 sts along right side of square 3. *Turn and k10, turn, k9, k last st tog with first st of square 4; rep from * until no sts of square 4 rem. Cut yarn.

Note Squares 11, 14, 15 and 18 are picked up from the sides of squares 1 and 4 in order to form the corners at the base of the bag. Your work will no longer lie flat after these squares are worked.

SQUARE 11
With B, pick up and k 10 sts from the right side of square 4. *Turn and k10, turn, k9, k last st tog with first st of square 10; rep from * until no sts of square 10 rem. Cut yarn.

SQUARE 12
Sl 10 sts of square 11 to LH needle. With D, pick up and k 10 sts from the right side of square 10. *Turn and k10, turn, k first st tog with last st of square 9; rep from * until no sts of square 9 rem. Cut yarn.

SQUARE 13
Sl 10 sts of square 12 to LH needle. With D, pick up and k 10 sts from the right side of square 9. *Turn and k10, turn, k first st tog with last st of square 8; rep from * until no sts of square 8 rem. Cut yarn.

SQUARE 14
Sl 10 sts of square 13 to LH needle. With spare needle, pick up and 10 sts from the cast on row of square 1. With C, pick up and k 10 sts from the right side of square 8. *Turn and k10, turn, k first st tog with last st of square 1; rep from * until no sts of square 1 rem. Cut yarn.
Cont as established, referring to placement diagram for color and direction of each square worked.

TOP TRIANGLES
With MC, pick up and k 10 sts from left side of square 50. *Turn, k10, turn, k9, k last st tog with first st of square 49; rep from * until no sts of square 49 rem. Sl

Jack Deutsch Studios

the 1 rem st to RH needle and bind it off over the first st picked up for the next triangle. Work 7 more triangles around top of bag. Bind off final st.

BAND
With RS facing and MC, pick up and k 10 sts across each triangle—80 sts. Pm for beg of rnd. Work in rnds of garter st (p 1 rnd, k 1 rnd) for 9 rnds. Bind off purlwise.

STRAPS (make 2)
With MC, cast on 120 sts. K 8 rows. Bind off purlwise.

FINISHING
Sew straps to bag (below band) at each point of side diamond.

FELTING
Work in all ends before felting. Place piece in a zippered pillowcase and put into washing machine. Use hot-water wash and a regular (not delicate) cycle. Add a tablespoon of laundry detergent and let the pieces agitate. Check the pieces frequently, agitating until desired felting is achieved; do no overfelt. Rinse in cold water and remove piece from pillowcase. Shape bag to finished measurements, then allow to air dry.

EVENING Bag

Jack Deutsch Studios

MEASUREMENTS
• Approx 10"/25.5cm wide x 8"/20.5cm high (excluding strap)

GAUGE
24 sts and 32 rows to 4"/10cm over St st.
Take time to check gauge.

STITCH GLOSSARY
Cluster 5 Sl next 5 sts to dpn and hold to front. Wrap yarn counterclockwise twice around these 5 sts. Place 5 wrapped sts on RH needle.

BAG
NOTES
1 Knit the first and last st of every row for selvage sts.
2 The stitch count changes from row to row.

BACK
Beg at bottom edge, cast on 73 sts.
Row 1 (WS) Knit. **Row 2** K1 (selvedge st), p71, k1 (selvedge st). **Row 3** Knit.
Row 4 K3, pm, k in front and back of next stitch, k21, pm, [yo, k22, pm] twice, k4—76 sts (23 sts between markers). **Row 5** K1, p3, *[p1, k3] twice, p1, k4, [p1, k3] twice, p2, rep; from * to last marker, end p2, k1. **Row 6** K3, *k1, yo, k1, [p3, k1] twice, p4, k1, [p3, k1] twice, yo; rep from * to last marker, end k4—82 sts (25 sts between markers). **Row 7** Keeping 1 st each side in garter st for selvedge sts, work rem sts as they appear, purling all yo's. **Row 8** K3, *[k1, yo] twice, [ssk, p2] 3 times, [k2tog, p2] twice, k2tog, yo, k1, yo; rep from *, end k4—76 sts (23 sts between markers). **Row 9** Rep row 7.
Row 10 K3, *[k1, yo] 4 times, [ssk, p1] twice, ssk, [k2tog, p1] twice, k2tog, [yo, k1] 3 times, yo; rep from *, end k4—82 sts (25 sts between markers).
Row 11 Rep row 7. **Row 12** K3, *k8, [ssk] twice, k1, M1, k1, [k2tog] twice, k7; rep from *, end k4— to last marker, k4—73 sts (22 sts between markers).
Row 13 Rep row 7. **Row 14** K3, *k9, Cluster 5, k8; rep from *, end k4—73 sts (22 sts between markers). Repeat rows 1–14 twice more, mark beg and end of last row for end of side seam, then rep rows 1-9 once.

Top shaping
Row 10 K3, k across dec 15 sts evenly spaced (dropping markers), end k4—58 sts. **Row 11** K1, p56, p1. **Row 12** K3, k across dec 9 sts evenly spaced, end k4—49 sts. **Row 13** K1, p47, k1.
Row 14 K3, *k5, Cluster 5, k4; rep from *, end k4—49 sts.

Rod pocket
Beg with a purl row, and keeping 1 st each side in garter st for selvedge sts, continue in St st for 4 rows. Knit next row for turning ridge. Beg with a knit row, cont in St st for 4 rows. Bind off.

FRONT
Work as for back.

FINISHING
Do not block.

LINING
Using bag back as a template, cut out two pieces of lining fabric ½"/1.3cm larger than curved edges and top straight edge even with turning ridge of rod pocket. Pin-mark at same points as row markers on bag. With RS tog, sew bottom seam and side seams to markers using a ½"/1.3cm seam allowance; set aside. With RS tog, sew back and front bag tog along bottom seam and side seams to markers; turn RS out. Fold each rod pocket over to WS along turning ridge and hem in place. Unscrew nut from each rod on frame, slip rod through rod pocket, then screw on nut. Wrap side edges of bag over to WS around side edges of frame; sew in place. Insert lining into bag. Turn all unstitched edges to WS so side edges butt side edges of bag and top edges butt bound-off edges at base of rod pockets. Slip stitch lining in place.

I-CORD HANDLES
With dpn, cast on 4 sts. Work I-cord over these 4 sts as foll: ***Next row (RS)** With 2nd dpn, k4, do not turn. Slide sts back to beg of needle to work next row from RS; rep from * until I-cord measures 24"/ 61cm. Bind off, leaving a long tail for sewing. Thread I-cord through handle eyelets, then sew ends of I-cord tog.

EYE POD Purse

MEASUREMENTS
• Approx 6"/15cm wide x 9"/23cm high (excluding strap)

GAUGE
15 sts and 21 rows to 4"/10cm over St st (before felting).
Take time to check gauge.

BAG
NOTE
Bag is made in one piece, beg at flap and ending at bottom edge of bag. Beg at botton edge of flap, with MC, cast on 31 sts. Work in St st for 36 rows.
Next row (RS) K1, M1, k30, cast on 30 sts for body of bag using backward loop method—62 sts. Beg with a p row, work in St st for 61 rows.
Bottom shaping
Row 1 (RS) K1, [k8, k2tog] 6 times, k1—56 sts.
Row 2 and all WS rows Purl.
Row 3 K1, [k7, k2tog] 6 times, k1—50 sts.
Row 5 K1, [k6, k2tog] 6 times, k1—44 sts.
Row 7 K1, [k5, k2tog] 6 times, k1—38 sts. Cont to dec in this manner, working 1 less st before the dec, every RS row until 14 sts rem, end with a WS row.
Next row (RS) K1, [k2tog] 6 times, k1—8 sts. Cut yarn leaving a long tail. Thread tail in tapestry needle and weave through rem sts. Pull tight to gather, fasten off securely, then sew side seam.

APPLIQUÉS
Square 1
With A, cast on 26 sts. Work in St st for 32 rows. Bind off.
Square 2
With B, cast on 18 sts. Work in St st for 20 rows. Bind off.

STRAP
With crochet hook and MC, loosely ch approx 84"/213cm. Fasten off.

FINISHING
FELTING
Work in all ends before felting. Place pieces in a zippered pillowcase and put into washing machine. Use hot-water wash and a regular (not delicate) cycle. Add ¼ cup of laundry detergent and an old towel or a pair of jeans for extra agitation. Check the pieces periodically to see if they are thick and the knit stitches are no longer visible. Rinse in cold water and remove pieces from pillowcase. Shape bag, tugging on flap until desired shape and rounding the bag's bottom. You may wish to stuff with plastic bags until dry. Dry remaining pieces flat.

APPLIQUÉS
Cut square A following template A and square B following template B. Position A appliqué on flap, then whipstitch edge in place using C. Position B appliqué in center of A, then position button in center of B. Working through all thicknesses, sew button using C. Using tip of knitting needle, poke a hole in each side of bag ¾"/2cm from top edge of bag, making sure it's large enough to accommodate strap. Thread each strap end through a hole from outside to inside (tweezers will be helpful to coax end through hole). Adjust for length, knot, then trim ends to neaten.

template

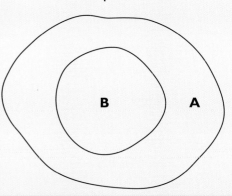

CENTRAL PARK Clutch

Jack Deutsch Studios

Rep rows 1 to 6 for slip st cable.

BAG
Cast on 58 sts. Work in St st for ¾"/2cm, end with a WS row. Purl next row on RS for turning ridge. Cont in diagonal scallop pat until piece measures 11"/28cm from turning ridge, end with row 4. K next row on WS for turning ridge. Cont in St st for ¾"/2cm. Bind off.

STRAPS (make 2)
Cast on 10 sts. Work in slip st cable for 14"/35.5cm. Bind off.

FINISHING
Block piece to measurements. Using bag as a template, cut out fabric lining ½"/ 1.3cm larger all around than bag. Turn fabric lining seam allowance ½"/1.3cm to WS; press. Slip stitch edge of lining to WS of bag. Fold purse hem to WS at each turning ridge and sew in place.

With RS facing, position straps 1¾"/ 4.5cm in from each side edge, with ends extending 3"/7.5cm above bound-off edge of bag; pin in place. At opposite end of each strap, place center of buckle under a strap, with prong through strap at 2½"/6.5cm from cast-on edge of bag and making sure that prong points toward top edge of bag; pin in place. Sew edge straps in place. With WS facing, fold cast-on edge up 4½"/11.5cm, leaving 2"/5cm free for flap. Sew side seams; turn right side out. Buckle straps.

YOU'LL NEED:

YARN ④
3½oz/100g, 220yd/200m of any worsted weight cotton blend

NEEDLES
One pair size 6 (4mm) needles *or size to obtain gauge*

ADDITIONAL MATERIALS
Two 1⅛"/3cm wide buckles, ½yd/.5m lining fabric, sewing needle, thread to match

MEASUREMENTS
• Approx 10"/25.5cm wide x 4¾"/125cm high

GAUGE
24 sts and 28 rows to 4"/10cm over diagonal scallop pat.
Take time to check gauge.

NOTES
1 Bag is made in one piece.
2 Straps are made separately and sewn on.

STITCH GLOSSARY
DIAGONAL SCALLOP PATTERN
(multiple of 4 sts plus 2)
Rows 1 and 3 (WS) Purl.
Row 2 K1, *insert needle from behind and lift the strand between the last st worked and the next st on LH needle, k2, then pass the strand over the 2 sts, k2; rep from *, end k1.
Row 4 K3, *insert needle from behind and lift the strand between the last st worked and the next st on LH needle, k2, then pass the strand over the 2 sts, k2; rep from *, end last rep k1.
Rep rows 1 to 4 for diagonal scallop pat.

SLIP STITCH CABLE
(worked over 10 sts)
Row 1 (WS) K2, p6, k2.
Rows 2 and 4 P2, sl 1 wyib, k4, sl 1 wyib, p2.
Rows 3 and 5 K2, sl 1 wyif, p4, sl 1 wyif, k2.
Row 6 P2, drop sl-st off needle to front of work, k2, then pick up sl-st and knit it (take care not to twist sl-st), sl next 2 sts to RH needle, drop next sl-st off needle to front of work, then sl the 2 sts back to left-hand needle, pick up dropped st with RH needle, replace it on the LH needle and knit it, k2, p2.

CABLED SHOULDER Bag

MEASUREMENTS
• Approx 14"/35.5cm wide x 15"/38cm high (excluding strap)

GAUGE
9 sts and 13 rows to 4"/10cm over St st.
Take time to check gauge.

STITCH GLOSSARY
6-ST CABLE
Row 1 (RS) K6.
Row 2 P6.
Row 3 Sl 3 sts to cn and hold to *front*, k3, k3 from cn.
Rows 4, 6 and 8 P6.
Rows 5, 7 and 9 K6.
Row 10 P6.
Rep rows 1 to 10 for 6-st cable.

BAG
BACK
Cast on 38 sts.

Beg cable pat
Row 1 (RS) K8, p2, k3, p3, work 6-st cable, p3, k3, p2, k8. **Row 2** P8, k2, p3, k3, work 6-st cable, k3, p3, k2, p8. Cont to work in this way until piece measures 16"/40.5cm from beg, end with a WS row.
Next row (RS) K8 and place these sts on holder for strap, k22, place rem 8 sts on holder for strap. Beg with a p row, work in St st over center 22 sts for 2"/5cm for facing. Bind off.

FRONT
Work as for back.

FINISHING
Block pieces to measurements. Sew side and bottom seams.

YOU'LL NEED:
YARN 6
17½oz/500g, 330yd/300m of any super-bulky weight wool blend

NEEDLES
One pair size 15 (10mm) needles *or size to obtain gauge*

ADDITIONAL MATERIALS
Cable needle (cn)
Stitch holders
1yd/1m lining fabric, sewing needle and thread to match

STRAP
With RS facing, k 8 sts from left back holder and 8 sts from right front holder—16 sts. Beg with a p row, work in St st for 20"/51cm. Bind off. Rep for other side of strap.

LINING
Fold lining fabric in half, RS facing. Trace body of bag onto lining fabric. Cut out pieces ½"/1.3cm larger all around. Using a ½"/1.3cm seam allowance, sew side and bottom seams. Turn top edge ½"/1.3cm to WS and press. Set aside. Trace one side of strap onto lining fabric. Cut out pieces ½"/1.3cm larger all around. Using a ½"/1.3cm seam allowance, sew one pair of short edges of strap lining tog. Turn all edges ½"/1.3cm to WS and press. Insert bag lining into bag. Slipstitch top edge in place. Fold 2"/5cm St st facings to WS and sew in place. Sew bound-off edges of knitted strap tog. Insert strap lining. Slipstitch short edges to top edge of body lining and long edges to strap.

Jack Deutsch Studios

WEEKENDER Bag

Jack Deutsch Studios

MEASUREMENTS
Bag
• Approx 16"/40.5cm wide x 15"/38cm high x 6"/15cm deep (excluding handles)
Large pocket
• Approx 10"/25.5cm wide x 11"/28cm high (after felting)
Small pocket
• Approx 5¾"/14.5cm wide x 6½"/16.5cm high (after felting)

GAUGE
13 sts to 4"/10cm over St st.
Take time to check gauge.

NOTES
1 Bottom of bag is worked back and forth on circular needle.
2 Body of bag is worked in the round.
3 Each row on chart is work from right to left.
4 Slip all sts purlwise.
5 Carry yarn not in use loosely across WS of all slipped stitches.

STITCH GLOSSARY
SLIP STITCH BODY PATTERN
Rnd 1 *K2, sl 2; rep from *, end k2.
Rnd 2 Knit.
Rnd 3 *Sl 2, k2; rep from *, end sl 2.
Rnd 4 Knit.
Rep rnds 1–4 for sl st body pat.

BAG
BOTTOM
With B, cast on 59 sts. Work back and forth in garter st for 34 rows. Bind off all sts knitwise.

BODY
With RS of bottom facing and B, pick up and k 58 sts along bound-off edge, 16 sts along side edge, 58 sts along cast-on edge and 16 sts along opposite side edge—150 sts. Join and pm for beg of rnds. Purl next rnd. Knit next rnd.
Beg chart pat I
Rnd 1 Work 10-st rep 15 times around. Cont to work chart in this way to rnd 10. With A, cont in sl st body pat for 4½"/11.5cm. Knit next 2 rnds.
Beg chart pat II
Rnd 1 Work 10-st rep 15 times around. Cont to work chart in this way to rnd 18. With A, cont in sl st body pat for 4½"/11.5cm. Work rnds 1–18 of chart pat II once more. With A, cont in sl st body pat for 4½"/11.5cm. Knit next rnd. Change to B and knit next 2 rnds.
I-cord bind-off
Working sts from circular needle to dpn, k4, k2tog tbl—5 sts on dpn. Cont I-cord bind off as foll: **Next row (RS)** *Slide sts to opposite end of dpn, with 2nd dpn, k4, k2tog tbl from circular needle; rep from * around until 5 sts rem on dpn and there are no sts rem on circular needle. Cut yarn leaving a long tail. Join I-cord ends tog.

LARGE POCKET
With B, cast on 40 sts. Work in St st and stripe pat of 4 rows B, 4 rows A until piece measures 17"/43cm from beg, end with a RS row. Knit next 2 rows with B. Bind off loosely.

SMALL POCKET
With B, cast on 22 sts. Work as for large pocket until piece measures 10"/25.5cm from beg, end with a RS row. Knit next 2 rows with B. Bind off loosely.

FINISHING
FELTING
Work in all ends before felting. Place pieces into washing machine. Use hot-water wash and a regular (not delicate) cycle. Add ¼ cup of laundry detergent and an old towel or a pair of jeans for extra agitation. Check the pieces periodically to see if they are nice and thick and the knit stitches are no longer visible. Rinse in cold water. Shape bag and pockets to measurements. Dry pieces flat. Position each pocket on WS of bag, so it is 2½"/6.5cm from top edge of bag and centered side to side. Sew in place using sewing thread. Sew on handles 3"/7.5cm down from top edge of bag.

MAT BOARD LINER
To cover mat board, cut two 7¼" x

LILYPAD Backpack

17¼"/18.5cm x 44cm pieces from fabric. With RS facing and using a ½"/1.3cm seam allowance, sew around three sides, leaving one short edge open. Turn RS out. Insert mat board. Fold open edge ½"/1.3cm to WS and whipstitch opening closed. Insert liner into bottom of bag.

BEADED ACCENT
Thread metallic yarn into tapestry needle. Thread on seed bead, 30mm bead, seed bead, 25mm bead, seed bead, 20mm bead, seed bead. Insert needle back through beads, skipping last seed bead. Even up ends of yarn. Thread both ends into tapestry needle. Sew securely to base of one handle on front as shown in photo.

Chart II

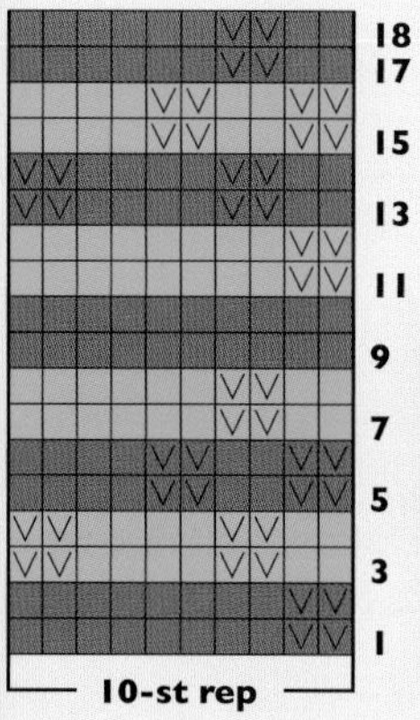

18
17
15
13
11
9
7
5
3
1

— 10-st rep —

Chart I

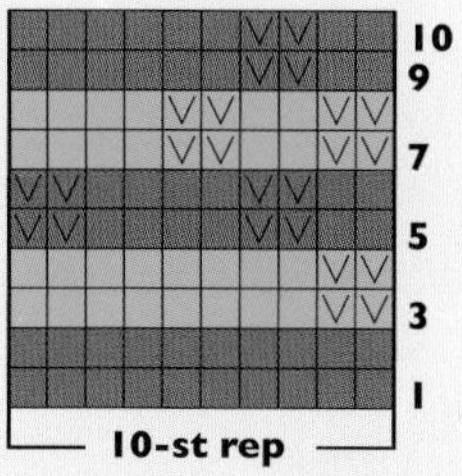

10
9
7
5
3
1

— 10-st rep —

Stitch Key
- Green Multi (A) Knit
- Green Multi (A) Sl 1 wyib
- Dark Brown (B) Knit
- Dark Brown (B) Sl 1 wyib

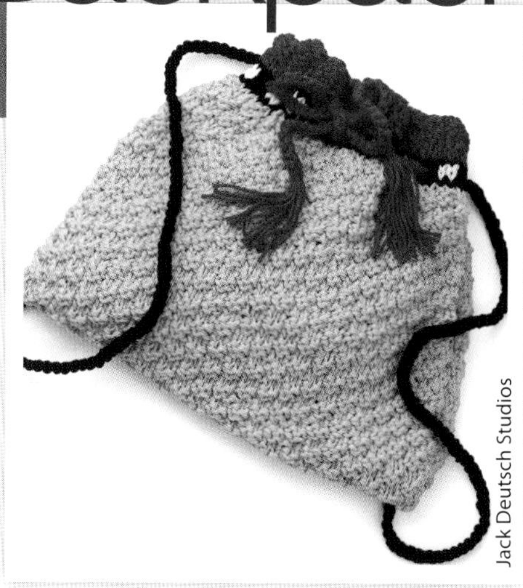

MEASUREMENTS
• Approx 9½"/24cm wide x 11½"/29cm high (excluding straps)

GAUGE
16 sts and 26 rows to 4"/10cm over double seed st using 2 strands of yarn. *Take time to check gauge.*

NOTES
1 Use 2 strands of yarn held tog throughout.
2 Bag is made in one piece, beg at back top edge and ending at front top edge.

STITCH GLOSSARY
DOUBLE SEED STITCH
(multiple of 4 sts)
Rows 1 and 2 *K2, p2; rep from * to end.
Rows 3 and 4 *P2, k2; rep from * to end.
Rep rows 1 to 4 for double seed st.

BAG
With 2 strands of A held tog, cast on 48 sts. Work in double seed st for 6 rows. Change to 2 strands of B. Purl next row.
Next row (RS) *K2 C, k2 B; rep from * to end.
Next row *P2 B, p2 C; rep from * to end. With B, knit next row.
Change to 2 strands of MC and purl next row. Cont in double seed st until piece measures 18"/45.5cm from beg, end with a WS row. With MC, knit next row.
Change to 2 strands of B, purl next row.
Next row (RS) *K2 C, k2 B; rep from * to end.
Next row *P2 B, p2 C; rep from * to end. With B, knit next row.
Change to 2 strands of A, purl next row. Cont in double seed st for 6 rows. Bind off.

FINISHING
Block piece to measurements. Fold piece in half, then sew side seams.

STRAPS (make 2)
With crochet hook and 2 strands of B,

Jack Deutsch Studios

make a ch 20"/51cm long. Fasten off. Sew one end to side seam, 1½"/4cm from top edge. Sew opposite end to back of bag, ½"/1.3cm from side seam and ½"/1.3cm from bottom fold.

DRAWSTRING
With crochet hook, 2 strands of A and leaving a long tail, make a ch 30"/76cm long. Fasten off leaving a long tail. Beg at center front, weave drawstring through B/C stripe at top edge of bag.

TASSELS (make 2)
Cut six strands of A, 7"/18cm long. Use crochet hook to draw ends of strands through one end of drawstring; even up strand ends. Wrap drawstring tail 3 times around tassel to secure strands, then fasten off tail securely.

BAG-Atelle

Dan Howell

YOU'LL NEED:

YARN 🄶
Hometown U.S.A. by Lion Brand Yarn Co., 5oz/140g skeins, each approx. 81yd/74m
4 skeins in #107 Charlotte Blue (MC)
1 skein in #194 Monterey Lime (CC)

NEEDLES
Size 15 (10mm) needles *or size to obtain gauge*

ADDITIONAL MATERIALS
Two purse handles
Cable needle (cn)
¼yd/.25m lining fabric
Sewing needle
Thread

Row 2 and all WS rows *K2, p4; rep from * to end.
Row 3 *P2, 4-st RC, p2, k4; rep from * to end.
Row 6 *K2, p4; rep from * to end.
Rep rows 1–6 until piece measures approx 23"/58.5cm, ending with a row 6. Bind off.

FINISHING
Fold work in half lengthwise, seam sides to 1"/2.5cm from top.
Place 1 handle at top of each side, fold 1"/2.5cm over each handle, sew to inside. With CC, make two pompons, one 2"/5cm and one 2½"/6.5cm. Make one 15"/38cm braid with MC. Attach pompons to each side of the braid and sew middle of braid to inside of purse, allowing pompons to dangle outside.

LINING
Cut piece of lining fabric to same measurements as purse. Fold fabric right side together, sew up sides. Fold top back 1"/2.5cm and hem. Hand-sew fabric lining into bag, sewing over handle bumps.

MEASUREMENTS
• 12" x 23"/30.5cm x 58.5cm

GAUGE
10 sts and 12 rows to 4"/10cm over cabled rib pattern.
Take time to check gauge.

STITCH GLOSSARY
4-st RC Sl 2 sts to cn and hold to *back*, k2, k2 from cn.

PURSE
With MC, cast on 34 sts.
Rows 1 and 5 (RS) *P2, k4; rep from * to end.